ABOUT THE AUTHOR

Jonathan Margolis is a technology journalist for the *Financial Times* and writes on more general subjects, especially China, for publications including the *Observer*, the *Guardian*, the *New Statesman* and the *Daily Mail*. He is a former London contributor to *TIME* magazine and is also the author of two popular science books – *The Intimate History of the Orgasm* and *A Brief History of Tomorrow*, an investigation into triumphs and disasters of futurologists through the ages.

The Secret Life of
URI GELLER

CIA MASTERSPY?

Jonathan Margolis

WATKINS PUBLISHING

LONDON

INTRODUCTION

I never planned to become an expert on Uri Geller. A smaller boy made me do it – my son, David, aged 15 in 1996, when we first had the Internet, became fascinated online by the controversy over Geller.

I sighed and tried to discourage him. 'He's just a washed-up fake,' I explained. David was not convinced, and through a wonderful British inventor, John Knopp, whom I had interviewed, he made contact with Geller.

Uri was soon inviting my whole family to come to his house. There was a slight setback when we turned up, all five of us, and Uri was out. His excuse was more than reasonable. He had been asked to go to the old Wembley Stadium to give some psychic support to the England football team.

We returned another week. We saw a spoon bend on its own, and a series of quite extraordinary micro events, enough to fill a long article in themselves, unfolded. This weird little pattern starts up again every time I have contact with Uri, even if I'm thousands of kilometres from him.

Now, intrigued, I began researching Uri, and found that everything I had told David – such as my absolute insistence that he had never been validated by science – was wrong.

Even so, Uri's life has been so packed with extraordinary, bizarre and fascinating incidents, and so rammed with stories, that 17 years after first meeting him, I'm still learning.

This book concerns a side of Uri that even many who know him well will not have been aware of until now. I think even the most sceptical reader will find it intriguing, and just possibly compelling.

Jonathan Margolis,
August 2013

Chapter One

A PHONE CALL

I t's a perfect spring day in 1981 in Stamford, Connecticut, just an hour or so north of New York City, yet more rural than suburban. A little way from the pretty town centre, you find yourself on Westover Road, passing the secluded, gated homes, mostly of wealthy New Yorkers who with their families have left the excitement of Manhattan (along with the less-missed muggers and garbage that typified the city in the '80s) for quiet, secluded, safe, green backyards and elite schools. Along on the right, there's a dirt track, rather grandly announced by the standard American white-on-green street sign as Long Close Road. Picking up a bit of dust as you go (the road today is paved and smooth, which almost detracts from its bucolic charm) this trail leads into a delightful forest, complete with lake. Along the way, so hidden as to be almost invisible, are even more desirable homes than on Westover.

In one of these, a large, imposing house built on a slope that gently dips down to a creek, lives a family, who, but for a few unusual details, of which we will hear more as this story

1

unfolds, typify the American dream of immigration gone extraordinarily right. The house, even back then, 35 years ago in the early days of Ronald Reagan's America, is worth close to a million dollars.

The Geller family, from Israel. There's 35-year-old Uri, who has made enough money to retire working as … well, we will get to that. There's his wife, Hanna, their two tiny children, Daniel and Natalie. There's Hanna's younger brother, Shipi, who has been Uri's best friend and, latterly, business partner since they were practically kids. And there's Uri's German-born widowed mother, Margaret, whom he has brought over from Tel Aviv to live in the States and be there for her grandchildren. It's an idealized, close, happy family set-up, which will remain unchanged for decades. Even today, with Margaret having died, Uri of retirement age, Daniel a successful attorney in Manhattan and Natalie an aspiring actress in Los Angeles, the Gellers are a stable, happy unit.

Back in 1981, the focus this particular sparkling morning switches over 640 kilometres to the south and to, of all places, the office of the newly appointed Director of the CIA, William Joseph Casey. Casey is 68, a New York Republican politician and devout Roman Catholic, with a wartime background in intelligence, for which he was awarded a Bronze Star. He has post-war experience as a lawyer, and a profound loathing and distrust of the Soviet Union. He was Ronald Reagan's campaign manager in his recent successful election and was one of the new president's key appointees.

We don't know what Casey has on his desk this morning a few weeks after he started as CIA director, when he phones Uri Geller in Connecticut. We don't know why he calls. We don't know why he doesn't get a subordinate at least to dial the number and announce that the Director of the CIA is on the line. But we do know the kind of material that had accumulated in Geller's bulging file over the ten years he has been a subject of interest to the Agency, so we can hazard an unusually informed guess.

Uri Geller had been brought to the CIA's attention in the early 1970s by the Israeli secret service, Mossad, and by a particular eccentric Serbian-American scientist, Dr Andrija Puharich, who had spent months in Tel Aviv if not at the explicit request of the CIA, then with its blessing, testing the young Israeli's apparently paranormal abilities with a view to both seeking to quantify and understand them – and to seeing if the young man had it in him to work covertly against the Soviet bloc.

The scientist had also been encouraged to investigate Uri Geller by the former Apollo astronaut Edgar Mitchell, the lunar module pilot on the Apollo 14 Moon landing. Mitchell had become the sixth man to walk on the Moon just a few months earlier, and had always had a scientific fascination with the paranormal. We will look back over the strange story of how Uri came to be in America at all later in this book. It is every bit as odd and intriguing – and disturbing – as the truly astonishing events that happened to and around the American intelligence community during the decade in the USA leading up to William Casey's out-of-the-blue phone call. These events seriously unhinged a considerable number of the hard-headed scientific researchers who investigated Uri. Some of them were never the same again – and not in a good way.

Yet the early indications seen by Andrija Puharich, the man the US government – or at least elements within it – nominated to investigate Uri, didn't suggest such an outcome. Far from it. Puharich, a polymath who had qualified as both a medical doctor and a physicist, had first seen Uri when the Israeli was working in a seedy nightclub. He struck the scientist as nothing more than an ordinary, not-very-good conjuror with an act consisting of a small number of effects – spoon bending, mind reading and stopping and starting clocks and watches – all of which could be replicated by any half-decent magician.

After months of work with Uri Geller in semi-laboratory conditions on his field trip to Israel, the scientist had changed his opinion radically. During the early 1970s, Uri (along with some other apparent psychics) went on to be the subject of formal experimentation in research in the USA funded by the CIA to the tune, we now know, of $20m. The most significant of these exhaustive tests had been done in 1972, by Stanford Research International (SRI), a big laboratory complex in Menlo Park, outside San Francisco. Their extraordinary success was widely reported after the CIA agreed to allow the lead scientists to write a largely positive report on Uri's mind-reading abilities for the prestigious British science journal *Nature* as a reward for their endeavours. It would do no harm if the Soviets got to read it, either.

All this, William Casey would have known from the file when he called Uri in 1981. The headline facts were not even secret; it is no exaggeration to say that Uri Geller was one of the most famous people in the world, a guest – bizarrely for someone being assessed for use as an espionage asset – on entertainment shows around the (non-communist) globe, a buddy of celebrities from John Lennon to Salvador Dali.

The Geller files – and we will see later a recently revealed extract from one of the documents that Casey will have had to hand – were also very clear on another thing about Uri Geller. That he was, and remains even today at the age of 66, an incorrigible, extrovert showman with a penchant for self-publicity – none of which, it goes without saying, suggests a man marked out by the CIA and other secret government agencies in the US, Israel, Mexico and possibly the UK for a life as psychic spy.

Psychic spy he most certainly was, as we will discover, but 'cool', in either the 1950s' and 60s' James Bond-ish mode that Casey would have understood, or in the more modern, dark espionage-fiction sense, Uri Geller most definitely was not. With examples of show business luminaries from Errol Flynn to Noël Coward known to have done their bit of intelligence work on the side, Geller saw no reason why he couldn't ride two horses and be both a celebrity and a spy. In his own field, almost, the great Harry Houdini had done just that in his day. Houdini's stunts made headlines, but also caught the eye of influential figures in US and British intelligence agencies.

A 2006 biography of the great Austrian-American stunt performer revealed that both the Secret Service and Scotland Yard hired him to infiltrate police stations in mainland Europe and Russia, keeping an eye out and an ear open for informative titbits. In return, Houdini demanded that the intelligence agencies help further his career. Before he would agree to spying assignments, Houdini insisted that William Melville, the head of the British Special Branch and later of the British Secret Service, who died in 1918, arranged for him to audition with London theatre managers.

Another important aspect of the Uri Geller story that would have featured high in his CIA case notes needs to be flagged up for the millions of those under the age of 35 or so and others who may be unacquainted with the known story of Uri Geller. That is that he was despised and derided, actively, vocally and with a vengeance, by many stage magicians and a substantial number of scientists, initially at home but later around the world.

To understand why Uri was the focus of such hatred, we must realize that conjurors specialize in performing feats for entertainment purposes that *look* like 'paranormal' or magical effects, but are actually produced by physical and mental trickery. They spend years honing and perfecting these tricks and were infuriated beyond imagining when Uri Geller cropped up in the 1960s saying the abilities he possessed were natural, that he had had them since early childhood and had no idea how he did what he did; it just 'kind of worked'.

The appearance of Uri Geller on the scene at the height of the hippy era, when rationalists were getting increasingly irritated by the boom in mysticism, was to prompt the growth of what might be termed 'professional scepticism'. All over the world, societies were founded and magazines published that cast an ever-cynical eye on all things mystic. What will be referred to in this story occasionally as 'the sceptics' tend to be dominated by an odd coalition of disgruntled stage magicians and scientists, atheists and devout ultra-rationalists, all with their own agendas. And 'the sceptics' have, in the minds of many educated people in different parts of the world, come to dominate the discussion that rages around Uri Geller and the paranormal. It is not the intention of this book to go too deeply into the 40-year argument between those who take Uri Geller and 'Gellerism' seriously and those who believe him to be a charlatan, but to let the evidence speak for itself and allow the reader to make a judgment call.

To make such a judgment, however, it is necessary to know – as one can be sure William Casey did – that the intellectual honesty of some of 'the sceptics' is far from a given. Most educated younger people tend to believe it is the sceptics who are the cowboys in white hats, when in reality a noisy minority are more like traditional Wild-West-movie, black-hat wearers.

To be fair, there are many honest, rigorous-minded people among the sceptics, who do not just sneer as an ill-considered kneejerk reaction. But more than a few journalists, lawyers and others – even former professional sceptics – have been surprised to discover a significant scattering of rogues amongst them. And the ranks of the organized, militant sceptics are, to this day, thick with rather over-emotional, excitable characters. Those on the fringes of this group are often, weirdly, superstitious. They are careless with accusations of fraud, engaging in multiple, documented cases in vicious personal attacks based on invented evidence. And they are notoriously reluctant even to read the research that challenges their prejudices. They are quick with fanciful conspiracy theories on how Uri and others do what they do – and, as with so many fundamentalists in various fields, fatally prone to falling out with one another.

One of the most prominent and public among the militantly anti-Uri Geller crusaders in the USA had been lobbying against Geller since the 1970s. Beyond question, his and other names will have been highlighted in Geller's case notes, now lying in front of William Casey: among them was a somewhat maverick character who had been exposed in a Baltimore court case as unreliable.

Decades later, indeed, when one reviews the strange, intense period most of this book covers, it is hard not to wonder, not only if Uri's loud, showy persona was a front, to make it impossible for anyone to believe he was engaged in serious espionage work, but also that the sceptics' ranks were riddled with CIA men, planted there to spread propaganda against Geller in an effort to convince the Soviets that the Americans' 'psychic secret weapon' was a fake, while in fact, significant elements among US intelligence were convinced that their mouthy Israeli superstar was absolutely the real thing. Andrija Puharich, indeed, believed the Defense Department decided that short of killing Uri, the best thing was to ridicule him, at least for public consumption, and that they effectively set up the sceptics' campaign. It's a theory, at least ...

The language of some the CIA's recently declassified (although heavily redacted) internal communications of the time – which again, not to labour the point, would have been available to Casey when he called Geller – strongly suggests, however, that the CIA considered Geller an extremely interesting potential asset.

One memo argues for taking Geller out of the hands of the semi-private SRI and getting him firmly under CIA control. Thus it proposes: '*Telling SRI (sincerely by the way) that we have no intention of easing them out and that they will have full access to the data and first option re publication, we persuade them to use their good offices with Geller in the following manner. They tell him that, in order to get the kind of money necessary for prolonged research, they showed the data and film on a highly selective basis to officials in the USG. [US government] While all expressed interest (and many incredulity) only one group had both the vision and the courage and the means to pursue the matter and they urge Geller to at least listen to the proposition they wish to make.*

'*If he asks who they represent,*' the document continues, '*SRI finesses the matter by telling him that the representatives themselves would rather explain their status. (NOTE: alternatively, with appropriate backstopping, we could pass ourselves off as NIH* [National Institutes of Health] *officials). SRI then provides the introduction to Geller and we try to convince him to accept a contract as a consultant for a two- or three-month period renewable if both parties concur. If we don't pose as NIH officials and if he insists on knowing who we are, we tell him but only after enough low-key and sympathetic exposure to permit him at least to judge us subjectively.*

'*If we pose as NIH, the rationale for our interest is simple – straight basic research. If we drop cover, the rationale is simply that in addition to our scientific interest in understanding the phenomena we are concerned about the potentialities for its use in the wrong hands and against the interests of humanity as a whole. We have a defensive responsibility in that regard and solicit his help in meeting it. In other words, we virtually level with him.*

'*As matters now stand we have little to lose and, handled adeptly, we might get a reasonably cooperative response. If so, we arrange for him to be ensconced in an NIH clinic (under alias if he prefers) and ensure that the conditions (privacy, security, yet freedom of movement for G, who will live and sleep there, but be free to leave outside "office" hours are optimum from his and our point of view.*

'*We then conduct the experiments designed for him and have him examined by an array of NIH specialists. In this context, while we probably have to keep the regimen as un-threatening and un-painful as possible, it would be great value if we could obtain blood/ metabolic/ other indices both when he is "high" (performing well) and when he is in a normal state. If consistent traces lead to biochemical suggestions, the whole matter of both identification and enhancement in others (drug-wise for example) might be short-circuited. All of us experience in less dramatic ways "on" and "off" states with minor cycles being measured in hours or days and major ones measured sometimes in years. When we are "on" we "click", feel fit and on top of things and we are perceived by others as being effective, dynamic magnetic etc. It seems reasonable to assume that similar or analogous cycles are operative in the "psi" arena and that (as with us) the underlying causes are physical/chemical as well as environmental/ psychological.'*

Another document sets out some of the reasons the CIA wanted to get its hands directly on the Israeli prodigy. '*It strikes me that what is of interest to CIA is not whether Geller's perceptions are sensory or extrasensory but rather whether his capabilities are exploitable by CIA (not necessarily utilizing Geller personally: possibly others could be trained to do what he does),*' it says. '*And indeed someone who could reproduce blueprints locked in safes without looking at the blueprints, or someone who could distinguish from a distance decoys from real missiles, would be an undoubted asset … SRI's experiments with Geller to date have dealt exclusively with behavioural tasks and not at all with examination of Geller himself (other than a cursory EEG examination which apparently revealed nothing abnormal) and future activities with him could deal with an examination of his perceptual abilities to learn whether e.g., his vision or hearing extends beyond normal human limits.*'

What we learn from the first of these typewritten documents (CIA-RDP96-00787B000400070025-6 for anyone keen to check it and others on the subject out personally) is nothing short of incredible. The spooks taking Uri Geller seriously in the early 1970s were not just the mavericks portrayed in the entertaining 2009 film starring George Clooney, *The Men Who Stare At Goats*, which was based very loosely on the events around (but not including) Uri Geller. They were real, memo-writing, career CIA spymasters. And so anxious were they to enlist Uri's powers that they plotted, if necessary, to pose as members of the US government's medical bureaucracy and appeal to his better nature, citing '*the potentialities for its use in the wrong hands and against the interests of humanity as a whole.*' The impression can hardly be avoided that, after his testing at SRI, Geller's powers were a given; to those in the know, they were not even up for discussion.

So what was the nature and substance of William Casey's call that morning in 1981? Well, it was nothing particularly heavy. In fact, it was curiously low key and informal – and brief. We have only Uri's story to rely on, but, as will emerge in due course, we have numerous accounts from other highly plausible sources – plus documents such as the ones above – to suggest that what Uri has said is most likely true and accurate. (He has also told the same story consistently to the author for the past 20 years. Its implications only became clearer in 2013, when the Oscar-winning BBC TV director Vikram Jayanti made his acclaimed 90-minute documentary *The Secret Life of Uri Geller*. It majored on detailed new revelations about Uri's espionage past, unearthed in interviews with witnesses who were only able to come forward with the passing of the years and the release of previously secret documents and programmes.)

But back to that call. The ringing phone was picked up by Uri's brother-in-law, Shipi. 'Hello,' Casey said. 'Am I speaking to Mr Uri Geller?' Casey, with Russians clearly on his mind, made the common mistake of pronouncing the Hebrew name 'Uri' as the quite different Russian name, 'Yuri'. Shipi, in his lugubrious way, asked to whom he was speaking; callers to the Geller property were self-selecting to some extent as the number wasn't listed. 'This is William Casey, Director, Central Intelligence Agency, calling from Langley, Virginia.'

'Uri,' called Shipi. 'It's the Director of the CIA.' He spoke in English rather than the Hebrew he would normally use with his brother-in-law. It was probable that Casey could tell that Shipi was smiling as he said this. Team Geller had been around spooks long enough to know that the Director of the CIA wouldn't normally make his own calls. It had also been at least a couple of years since Uri had been involved in any intelligence work. What could this be about? Uri took the call anyway. 'Hello, this is Uri Geller,' he said, his voice disarmingly lighter than Shipi's, making him sound a little younger. Casey again politely introduced himself, explained that he was new in post and was acquainting himself with a few ongoing matters of interest.

'Sir, I don't like to sound rude or sceptical,' Uri said, 'but could you please tell me some more about what you know about me. I am sure you are who you say you are, but you will excuse me if I say you could be anybody, You will understand that I have to be a little bit careful.' Casey was remarkably patient for an older man who was used to people jumping at his command, especially since he had been in his elevated new role. But he gave a few details about the programme at SRI almost a decade earlier, naming the key scientists involved, Dr Hal Puthoff, a laser physicist, and Russell Targ, a specialist in plasma physics, as well as several lesser-known researchers.

Uri was soon convinced. 'OK, so how may I help you, Mr Casey?'

It turned out that the Director was merely curious to do a little ESP test personally. 'Mr Geller,' he said. 'I'm sitting at my desk at CIA. Can you tell me what I'm holding in my hand right now?' Uri thought about this for a minute or so, as he recalls, although he concedes that it may not have been that long – a minute is a very long silence in a phone call, especially one with a complete stranger who happens to be one of the most important people in the USA. Eventually, he said, 'I can't be sure, but my feeling is that it's a dagger with a white, possibly ivory, handle.' It was Casey's turn to be silent now. 'Well, I'll be darned,' he finally said, thanked Uri for his time and was not heard from – directly – again.

* * *

The reasons for William Casey's 1981 call to Uri Geller can never be known. He died six years later and so far as we know, never confided in anyone. Maybe it was just a bit of curiosity on his part during an idle moment at work; maybe he did it because he could; maybe simply because he had the power in his new job to call up Uri Geller on a whim. Nonetheless, it seems no small thing for the head of the world's leading intelligence agency to have taken time out to satisfy such a whim if such it was, right in the middle of an escalating Cold War. One can only speculate beyond the bald facts. There was no obvious, immediate consequence so far as anyone in a position to say so knows.

The high point of the extraordinary spy story around Uri had, after all been concentrated on that key early 1970s' period. So let us now spool back to that time, through the eyes of several of the key people involved, especially the ones who first came to light in Vikram Jayanti's documentary. In later chapters, we will add many layers of detail to the story, and look at the equally fascinating build-up to Uri Geller's American adventures, as well as the many sequels.

The most important new voice to emerge publicly – the biggest piece by far in the jigsaw one has to assemble to get a true picture of Uri Geller's hidden, below-the-line life as a spy – is that of one Kit Green. Green was the CIA contract monitor who oversaw the research into Uri and other psychics who were examined – albeit at arm's length, via Puthoff and Targ at SRI – in the spy establishment's quest to explore unorthodox methods of countering the perceived threat of the Soviet Union.

Chief amongst these methods was 'remote viewing' – using psychics with ESP to 'observe' Soviet military installations from thousands of kilometres away. It was understood that the Soviets were experimenting with the same potential method of espionage, and indeed were far more advanced with it. Kit Green, who was a PhD medical scientist in his early 30s at the time, was identified by name only in the Jayanti documentary; his current role and location were not specified. But when approached for this book, Green the spymaster decided to come in still further from the cold.

Kit Green is truly the man who knows. At the CIA, where he gave the green light to the American psychic 'remote-viewing' programme, that started with Uri Geller and became a 20-year research project called 'Stargate', this remarkably multi-faceted scientist was the Agency's Branch Chief for Life Science in the Office of Scientific Intelligence. By the early 1980s, he was the Senior Division Analyst and

Deputy Division Director, as well as being Assistant National Intelligence Officer for Science and Technology. After leaving the CIA, he became Chief Technology Officer for General Motors in Detroit – and then qualified as a medical doctor!

Today, aged 73, Dr Christopher C. Green, to give him his full name, is a Professor of Diagnostic Radiology and Psychiatry at Detroit Medical Center and Assistant Dean at Wayne State School of Medicine, the largest medical school in the USA. In 2011, he addressed the Royal Society in London, the world's oldest scientific fellowship, at a conference on 'Applications of Neuroscience for Policy and Threat Assessment,' with particular reference to the enhancement, manipulation or degradation of human performance. His actual address was entitled, *Neuroscience Applications for Militaries, Intelligence and Law Enforcement*. It argued that medical scientists must remain aware that, with the explosion of discoveries in the area of neurosciences, will come individuals, political entities and countries, all seeking to exploit those findings for their own, nefarious purposes.

Curiously, perhaps, since Kit Green began to figure more and more in Uri's strange double life in the USA in the 1970s, both before and after Uri came to learn that Green was a CIA official, Green was never known to Geller by his real name. Until recently, to Uri, he was 'Rick', his CIA contact. And to this day, the two have never met.

This, then, is how Kit Green remembers first hearing of Uri in 1972.

'One afternoon, I got a telephone call at my desk, in the headquarters building. And the phone call initially was on what we called "the red line", a classified line. It was an intelligence agency of a very powerful ally of the United States of America, and they were troubled because a member of their military, an enlisted man, was doing things for them that they couldn't understand that appeared to have an electromagnetic aspect. He was capable of altering highly sophisticated electronics, which included imaging electronics, at will. And they didn't know how he was doing it. The question was simply, "Can you help us?" My response initially was, "Of course, I'll be glad to try." I was very interested as an electrophysiologist and neurophysiologist, not as a physician initially. And that was what I was initially asked about. The word "psychic" didn't appear for a long time with Geller.'

It was some months before Uri, for he it was who was the subject of the phone call, finally made it into Puthoff and Targ's safe hands at SRI, the CIA having seen to it that what was being done did not look overtly as if it was in any way a CIA project. But when the tests on Geller were underway, Green's phone was soon ringing again. 'Within a very short period of time, a week or ten days, I had a call at headquarters. It was the chief scientist at the Stanford Research Institute and he was talking about other aspects of Uri Geller's capabilities. I of course said, "Well, what other kinds of things are you talking about?" And without much of a pause the scientist said, "Well, he says he can see things at a distance." And I said, "No, he can't." And they said, "Yes, he can – and he's right here." So I said, "Hi, Uri. Well what can you see?"

Hal Puthoff explains today that Uri was kept in the dark about who was on the phone, because the pretence had to be maintained that the Virginia-based CIA was not involved in any way with the laboratory testing in distant California. As we saw in the CIA document above, the Agency was nervous not only about the news leaking prematurely that they were

Physicist Hal Puthoff, one of the first scientists to test Geller at Stanford Research Institute, California.

working, albeit through a third party, with psychics, but that Uri would be upset if he thought he was working for the CIA. They were not to know that working in espionage had been his dream since he was a boy, and that he would have seen coming to America to work for the CIA after his connections with Mossad back home (of which more later) was akin to being promoted to a big league from a lower division. So Uri was simply told on the call with Green that he was 'a scientific colleague on the East Coast' who was curious about his remote-viewing capability.

'So,' continues Dr Green, 'I turned and picked up a book, a collection of medical illustrations of the nervous system, and I opened it up to a page and I just stared at it. And Uri said, "Oh, I'm seeing something kind of strange." Uri, Puthoff recalls, scribbled something and crumpled it up, did the same again, and finally said, "Well, I don't know what to think. It looks like I have made a drawing of a pan of scrambled eggs. Yet I have the word 'architecture' coming in strong.'"

What astonished Green – to the extent that he went on to get authorization for the $20m programme that would become 'Stargate' – was that the illustration on the page he had 'shown' Uri was a cross-section of the human brain. 'But what caught my attention was that I had written across the top of his drawing the words "architecture of a viral infection". I had been looking at the biological warfare effect on the nervous system of a threat virus.

'They then did tremendous analysis to see if there was any chance that there were any cues over the telephone lines and so on,' Puthoff says today. 'But that was a genuine result. There are others like that that we did that we've never published. But it certainly convinced us that he has ability.'

Fascinated by the impromptu experiment in the office, Kit Green, the archetype of the sceptical scientist (sceptical in the sense of inquiring, not merely dogmatic) resolved to redo it – unannounced and from home – at the weekend. Certain things were still troubling him about the approach from SRI. Unlikely as it was, perhaps he had been fooled; the folks at SRI had, after all initiated the test by calling him. What if it had been the other way round?

'So I did an experiment in which I established myself and some documentary materials, including some numbers written on paper by a colleague and sealed in an envelope and then in another,' Dr Green relates. 'And I arranged to do this experiment in my home as an unclassified project with no forewarning to him. Although it was the weekend, the team at SRI happened to be there when I called, and I asked if Uri could describe the unspecified item. I had put the double envelope up on a music stand in my den.

'Two things occurred along with him reading the numbers correctly, as I established when I broke the seals and opened the envelopes. While he was "viewing" them, I moved the documents from one position to another inside the envelopes; I went over and lifted the outer envelope while I was on the phone and turned it through 180 degrees because it was upside down. And he became very upset while I was doing it. Actually, he started to scream and asked, "What happened? What did you just do? I'm getting nauseous, I want to vomit." When I explained, he said, "Please don't do that again because I was reading when you rotated it." But then after that he said something else had happened and wanted to know if I was all right.

'I said, "Slow down. I'm sitting upstairs in my den at my home, in northern Virginia, it's a beautiful day, my family's downstairs, what are you talking about? He said, "OK, Rick. For reasons I can't explain, something happens and I get suffused with an incredible amount of information, which in some cases is very disturbing, and I just now received a strange picture and event. I had a picture of glass shards fracturing and going through a body and pain as it went through, and in the background I saw a square-headed dog that was completely white with blood coming down from the dog's neck onto the floor, which was a sea of green. I didn't know what that meant and I was worried because it was while we were having our conversation."

'About an hour later, we finished and I went downstairs into our family room, which we'd moved all the furniture out of a few hours before to have a new green carpet laid down. And my family had put in the room on the new carpet a tall pole lamp with a huge glass shade and it had shattered all over the carpet. I found the family and asked what happened.

'They said that about an hour ago, Charles, our snow-white English bulldog – with a square head – had run into the room, got tangled in the cable and pulled the lamp over. And my mother the week before had macraméd a huge, wide, bright-red collar to go around the bulldog's neck. And it had been the collar that twisted round the cable. Now when I've reported this in the past,' says Dr Green, 'people have said, "So what. It's an anecdote". And I say, "Sure it's an anecdote, an uncontrolled experiment, but it happened to me." And it was too far away in the house for me to have heard the crash.'

Did such incidents not severely challenge the rationality of a young scientist, already in a plum position in the CIA and clearly destined to go places? 'I did find it disturbing intellectually because there was no way I could explain it from a materialistic perspective,' Green says. 'What we now know, many years later, is that there is a theoretical framework, which is quantum entanglement, which is the way in which brains communicate internally and externally. So at the time, I found it scientifically intriguing, but not a counterintelligence issue, because I know darned well I was not being spied on in my home, or that they were looking into my home with cameras or something. Because they didn't know I was going to be having this conversation until a minute or two before when I picked up the phone and called.'

So since those strange, unsettling episodes happened to him personally, how does Dr Green feel when he hears magicians and sceptical fellow scientists say all such things are simple magicians' tricks and of no scientific interest? 'That kind of comment comes from people who don't know, who will read something by a magician and they'll look at this and hear it said that Geller did this or that.

'But the fact of the matter is that that isn't correct. Anybody who has studied Geller and seen what he does and the films of what he does recognizes that there are profound differences between what Geller does and magicians' tricks. There's not even a remotely qualified individual who's ever investigated Geller who believes this orthodoxy – that it's all trickery – has any value. It does not.

'There's another issue, too,' says Kit Green. 'Many of the individuals who have been making a living out of debunking Geller are intellectually and morally bankrupt individuals. The RV [remote-viewing] experiments for me were astonishing. He was a superb remote viewer. He was a superstar. It is sometimes asked why, since he was so good at remote viewing, he wasn't officially in our elite group of remote viewers, and the reason for that is that it was his physics characteristics that were being researched very profoundly in a lot of laboratories, including government facilities. He was under review principally because he was of interest in the physics and materials science – the things that inexplicably it appeared he could do interacting with materials and electronics. In other words, we already had some outstanding remote viewers and needed Uri Geller for other, potentially even more important, matters.'

Let's try, then, because it will be mentioned again, to get a handle on the quantum entanglement theory, which is essence, what Dr Green is talking about when he mentions the interaction of materials and electronics. A warning first, though; because quantum physics or quantum mechanics involves phenomena which even scientists describe as 'weird' or 'spooky', it has become a bit of a mantra for non-scientists to put anything unusual, from ghosts to strange coincidences down to quantum physics. This causes some scientists to get extremely heated and dismissive about what they call 'woo woo' science. It's notable, by the way, that Uri never tries to invoke quantum as an explanation for his abilities, but plenty of his supporters do, and if they're not knowledgeable about quantum physics, they probably do him a disservice by making it easy for scientists to scoff.

The problem, however, is that scientists are not of one mind and love nothing better than tearing into one another and calling each other idiots who know nothing about what quantum *really* is. They do this either in scholarly articles – or more often in emotional emails and statements to one another. This squabbling and bitching has been going on since the 1930s, when quantum theory was first developed, and it is not a pretty spectacle to anyone who likes to think – as do a lot of the professional sceptics who hate Uri Geller – that science has definitive, black-and-white answers to everything.

The reality is that, and this really is not using over-emotive language, that quantum entanglement – which broadly speaking involves separate sub-atomic particles affecting one another more or less instantaneously whether they are centimetres or light years apart – is probably the most mysterious phenomenon we know of in the universe. We are talking here about separate, distant objects behaving like one entity, while remaining two separate objects. Additionally, although 'non-locality', as quantum entanglement is also often called, has been demonstrated regularly in laboratories since the 1990s and is already being exploited in real-life applications in electronics and other fields, not even the most knowledgeable scientist has much of a clue how it works.

One quantum theory pioneer, the Princeton physicist, John Wheeler, said if you are not completely confused by quantum mechanics, you do not understand it, while the great theoretical physicist Richard Feynman famously said that nobody understands quantum mechanics and that if anyone tells you they know how it works, they're lying.

Even Einstein, who was partly responsible for describing quantum theory, was disturbed by aspects of it from the start. The non-locality in particular troubled him: he described it as 'spooky action at a distance'. His issue was that if particles could act in concert almost instantaneously from one side of the Universe to the other, information (or whatever it is) would need to be travelling faster than light, which his own work argued was an impossibility. (How much faster than the speed of light quantum entanglement provably works might have spooked Einstein still further; in one recent experiment, physicist Nicolas Gisin of the University of Geneva measured photons – light particles –18 kilometres apart apparently sending information to one another at 10,000 times faster than the speed of light. 'I want to be able to tell a story,' Professor Gisin has said, 'and I cannot tell you a story of how nature manages the trick.')

So in quantum theory we have sub-atomic particles entangled, in the sense of being 'tied together', affecting one another and seemingly communicating at absurd speeds. We have the prospect, any year now, of quantum computers using quantum effects, even though these can't be explained, to work millions of times faster than today's electronic computers.

Entanglement is also the basis of teleportation, which is no longer 'Beam-me-up-Scotty' science fiction, since it has been demonstrable in the laboratory since 1997, four years after it was first seriously proposed. In teleportation, two quantum-entangled objects seem to act in concert as a link that moves information from one physical location to another. Chinese researchers currently hold the official record for teleportation distance, having teleported a piece of information via entangled photons across 16 kilometres of urban landscape and a lake.

But what does all this have to do with Uri Geller, mind reading, ESP, remote viewing and metal bending, not to forget ghosts, poltergeists, and even while we're at it, the placebo effect, mind-over-matter, Jungian synchronicity, chanting, prayer, miracles and religion?

Obviously, broadly speaking, everything 'paranormal' from spoon bending to prayer power is in the same ballpark as thought transference. But there has been no experimental work on the mechanics of how any of this might be working. So far, photons are the main things to have been provably entangled, although the size of demonstrably entangled objects is slowly increasing; in various experiments, a blob of thousands of photons and even a centimetre-long crystal have reportedly been entangled with a photon. And nothing experimental has (yet) demonstrated anything remotely involving brain cells swapping information via quantum entanglement. Yet we have globally respected scientists like Dr Green in Detroit and other researchers who are not even notably 'heretical', explicitly stating that the explanation for the abilities of Uri Geller and his like is most likely quantum entanglement.

And there are tantalizing glimpses of what you might call Geller-like aspects within what is known about entanglement. One such hint is the puzzling fickleness and unreliability of entanglement. It is famously finicky, declining and even disappearing abruptly – something known as 'entanglement sudden death' – with even slight external disturbance. 'Gellerism', to coin a phrase, is similarly unpredictable and often weak and indeterminate. Sceptics love to hoot with laughter at Uri's not-uncommon inability to 'perform', especially when he is surrounded by people who want him to fail. These sceptics, though, don't appear to find it odd that people in the public eye, from comedians to athletes to politicians, seem to do better with an audience willing them on, and often flop with a crowd that's against them, but we'll let that pass.

In conventional science, however, effects are meant to be consistent on all occasions, in all conditions, regardless of the experimenter's feelings. Yet amongst its oddities, a particularly peculiar part of quantum entanglement is that an observer can affect an entangled system; yes, merely *measuring* one object that is entangled with another can cause the state of the distant object to change to that of the one being measured. Indeed, even emotions can, in this field, affect outcomes. No wonder, perhaps, that sceptical scientists by and large shun this kind of research on the somewhat unscientific grounds that it just can't be true!

There are other fragments of the work in progress that is the understanding of quantum entanglement, which hint at Gellerism and the whole gamut of weird science. Some research suggests that everyday objects are so made that their components are entangled not just with each other but also with almost everything with which they have interacted throughout their existence.

To those who like to think (woo woo) of the Universe in holistic terms, this is most interesting. There are also tantalizing, though unconfirmed, theories emerging that quantum entanglement may not be limited to physics, but might also appear in living systems. Some research suggests, for example, that migrating birds use quantum effects unwittingly (OK, it wouldn't be wittingly) to increase their sensitivity to the Earth's magnetic field, possibly by entangling the electrons of cryptochrome, a light-sensitive molecule believed to be involved in avian navigation.

It is all still some journey that starts from the basis of photons acting in cahoots across laboratories and finishes with a proposal that neurons in separate brains might be able to fire one another remotely. It is an even longer journey before you arrive at quantum entanglement as a theoretical framework for the reason why the molecules in a spoon should change in nature as a result of Uri Geller being in the vicinity and putting on his cross, concentrating face. Yet the fact that serious scientists protective of their reputations willingly associate themselves with the notion – indeed not just associate with it, but take it out for dinner and invite it to stay over – that the paranormal abilities of Uri Geller and others are down to quantum entanglement or something like it can surely not be ignored.

Chapter Two

LAB RAT

Even before it became known that Uri Geller had an intriguing and fascinating past – and an intriguing and fascinating present, too – as someone definitely involved in espionage on behalf of three nations (Israel, the United States, Mexico) and possibly a fourth (the United Kingdom) one of the most common questions asked about him by those curious to know more about this unusual media personality and fixture of British life, is usually expressed as something like, 'Yes, but has he ever been tested by science?'

That Uri is in his 60s, yet looks to be in his 40s, has been friends with the likes of Michael Jackson and John Lennon and lives in a fine mansion on one of the most exclusive stretches of the River Thames in Berkshire, is still generally well known. That he is famous for being able to bend spoons and interfere with old-fashioned, mechanical watches by some disputed form of mental power is, these days, possibly a little less well known, his mind-reading ability, less so still.

Even less known, indeed practically *un*known, is the fact that he has been tested and validated by some of the most rigorous and protracted research ever unleashed on one individual. Even where this is known, it tends to be disbelieved, or its results reported falsely. This is only partly because the waters have been deliberately muddied by the orchestrated sneering of the ubiquitous, closed-minded – yet undeniably fashionable – lobby occupied by professional sceptics. A lot of ignorance about Uri Geller's true scientific background is simply the result of his heyday dating back to another, monochrome, naïve era, to a feeling that we have 'moved on' and become less gullible and more sophisticated.

And yet the details of what happened around Uri back then more than stand up to the test of time. They actually amount to some of the more fascinating scientific history on record – along with, as we will see shortly, some of the spookiest accounts given by reliable witnesses of what can only be called X-Files-type events.

'I'd never bought an ESP journal or ever subscribed to *Fate* magazine,' says lead investigator Hall Puthoff, laughing, as he looks back on why he accepted the challenge of working with Uri Geller at the Electronics and Bioengineering unit of Stanford Research Institute in 1972. 'No, I wasn't interested at all. In fact, as it turns out, the only reason I got involved in this was that I was interested in what we now call quantum entanglement. I said at the time, "OK, here's something that apparently occurs. So, there must be some physics here. So, let's take a look at it." To a physicist, if it moves, it's physics.'

Puthoff had early indications, however, that he and his colleague Russell Targ would be examining someone who was rather more than a nightclub magician, as Uri had been when

Targ's doctor/physicist friend Andrija Puharich first saw him in Tel Aviv. 'Behind the scenes,' Puthoff explains today, 'we were approached by Israeli Intelligence and they had been working with Geller in Israel.

'But they had only been doing operational things; they had not had any chance to do anything scientific. So they asked us if we would be willing to share with them whatever we found out in a scientific venue. That wasn't my call. So that was up to the CIA if they wanted to do that.' (The programme, originally funded by the CIA, was later passed on to its military equivalent, the DIA. But, as Russell Targ says today, 'The whole government was aware. We were supported by the CIA, Defence Intelligence Agency, Army Intelligence and NASA.')

Kit Green, known officially to all as 'Rick', the CIA contract monitor, was concerned, as were Puthoff and Targ, that the young Israeli delivered to them could be a fraud. The Mossad had been candid with Green that their conclusion from their experience with him in Israel was that Geller was a potentially powerful military weapon who had proved himself useful in secret military tests, but at the same time, as a flamboyant show business personality, in terms of keeping a secret, he was likely to be about as discreet as a giant megaphone. Their recommendation to the Americans, therefore, was to test him and use him, with their compliments as it were, but to be careful. Israel, for its part, was letting the USA take a look at Geller in exchange for use of American spy satellites as they passed over the Arab countries.

Part of the preparation at SRI was to eliminate any chance that Uri might be using standard magician's effects. The scientists were well aware that however qualified they were in their field, it was still possible to be fooled by magicians expert in theirs. To this end (and despite the fact that Targ was a keen amateur magician who was a regular in the magic shops on 42nd Street in New York and prided himself on knowing well the field of professional magic) several stage magicians were drafted in to SRI, both to pose as lab assistants and to review frame-by-frame video tapes of Geller at work. One such was an expert of the day in psychic magicianship called Christopher Evans and even he confessed on many occasions that he could not work out how Uri could be doing what he did.

None of this convinced the most devout sceptics, of course. Among their more implausible conspiracy theories was one that in the course of his own preparations for SRI, Uri had had

Physicist Russell Targ who carried out experiments with Uri Geller, Stanford Research Institute, California, USA.

a radio fitted in a tooth, by means of which Shipi, the Mossad or possibly the Tooth Fairy herself, could communicate with him; even though one of the most prominent anti-Geller magician activists, a Canadian-born performer called James Randi, conclusively trashed the tooth radio notion in an open letter to the British Magic Circle magazine *Abracadabra*, it is still occasionally touted on the Internet.

It is an attractive but ultimately not-quite plausible idea. For one thing, SRI was alert to all sorts of possibilities for fraud, some kind of radio scam amongst them. Uri was duly shielded by a radioproof Faraday cage. In Britain, *New Scientist* magazine, possibly peeved that SRI had gone to its rival *Nature* with the Geller report, cleverly unearthed patents Andrija Puharich had filed back in the 1960s for a variety of tooth radios. The significant point, however, was that these projects were never built; the electronic components for anything workable simply didn't exist. As a sensible precaution, however, Uri submitted himself for an examination with a prominent New York dentist, Dr John K. Lind, who was a full clinical professor at Columbia University, and in his private capacity looked after Greta Garbo's, Errol Flynn's, Arthur Miller's and Marilyn Monroe's teeth. 'I can attest to the fact that clinical and radiographic examination of Geller's mouth, teeth and jaws reveals no foreign objects implanted such as transistors, metal devices, etc.' Dr Lind reported in a statement.

Another amusing example of the sceptics' near-panic at the spectre of Uri Geller being taken seriously was when, under the auspices of another government agency (ARPA, the Pentagon's Advance Research Projects Agency), they managed to get a renowned sceptical psychologist who was also a skilled magician to observe the SRI tests for a day. Using his trained eye, he reported back, without being specific, on all kinds of areas in which it was probable Geller was fooling SRI. Unfortunately, his observational expertise also led him to state in his report that Geller's eyes are blue; they are, in fact, brown. So much for the trained eyes of the sceptical.

Uri Geller had finally got to the SRI at the end of 1972. The rumour that he was going to be tested at such a prestigious establishment had spread throughout a bemused scientific world, not to mention an incandescent conjuring fraternity. Uri knew that how he performed at SRI would be crucial to his future in the States, and that a failure here would almost certainly wipe him out worldwide, as well as bury forever, the fledgling academic study of *psi* – the blanket term for all forms of parapsychology and the paranormal.

The pressure on Geller was immense. He knew that he was genuine, but if he failed to convince the scientists testing him that he was not some sort of clever charlatan who had managed to contrive ever more clever ways of covering his tracks in ARPA's fully fledged laboratory setting, he would be finished. His reputation in Israel, especially among the intelligence community there, which he had been assiduously courting (and they him) in his efforts to fulfil his childhood dream of being a spy, would be in tatters.

Uri, Shipi and Dr Puharich were met at San Francisco Airport by Edgar Mitchell, Dr Wilbur Franklin of Kent State University's Physics Department, who was interested in him, and Puthoff and Targ. Puthoff at the time was a senior research engineer at SRI and held patents in the field of lasers and optical instruments. He was also co-author of *Fundamentals of Quantum Electronics*, a textbook on the interrelation between quantum mechanics, engineering and applied physics. He had been a lieutenant in naval intelligence, handling the highest category of classified material, a civilian operative of the National Security Agency, and was involved in the early 1960s in the development of ultra-fast computers for military use.

Targ, meanwhile, was a senior research physicist and an inventor, who had been a pioneer in the development of lasers, and had a series of abstruse laser devices, such as the tuneable plasma oscillator and the high-power gas-transport laser, to his name. He had built a laser-listening device for the CIA to 'get information from distant places' as he puts it guardedly. Targ had sought out Puthoff for two reasons when he heard that he was doing high-level research into psychics. The first was that he already had an interest in psychic research, the second, his fascination with magicianship.

SRI had been part of the neighbouring Stanford University since 1946, but had become an independent think tank, laboratory and problem-solving organization in 1970. Its 2,800 staff members worked in 100 different disciplines on the 28-hectare site in Menlo Park and other offices around the USA and overseas. The Institute worked on contract for both private industry and government, including secret defence work. But the fact that the client for the investigation into Uri Geller (as well as other psychics who were examined as part of the same programme) was the CIA remained a closely held secret until recently. Back in the early 1970s, the cover story was that the work was sponsored by a foundation Edgar Mitchell had established, along with a paranormal investigation group in New York.

Uri's testing took place in two parts, the first in late 1972, and the remainder in March 1974. Once it was clear that the Israelis were monitoring the SRI tests, the security around Geller increased. 'We were doing our own security as SRI, but we were reporting to the CIA, and they wanted to be sure that we were taking every possible precaution,' recounts Puthoff.

'We were stationing people on the top of SRI buildings looking for people on the top of other SRI buildings. We did all kinds of things. Another concern was that he was working for Israeli intelligence, and that they were just out to prove that he was a superman in order to scare the Arabs, and that therefore he might be something like the Six Million Dollar Man. He might have a whole shadow team with eavesdropping equipment. So we tore apart the ceiling tiles every evening looking for bugs. Our concern that this was an intelligence plot resulted in our paranoia being much deeper than the typical sceptic would demand.'

Of course, trying to fool Uri Geller is not easy, as Puthoff noticed. 'He is one of the brightest people I have met. He is very quick on the uptake, he doesn't miss a thing, and for those who would say that he is a magician pure and simple, he certainly sees things that the ordinary person doesn't. We might walk by a laboratory where I had a couple of agents hidden in the back with 30 other people, and Uri would walk by and point to them and say, "Who are those two guys?" As far as I could tell, they looked just like everybody else.'

Along with salting the laboratory with undercover conjurors, Puthoff and Targ had also taken advice on the kind of conditions that might help psychics to perform. 'They tried to make the environment very homely,' Uri says. 'They had a living-room setting with paintings on the wall and all those at-home kind of features so that I would feel good. But outside, they had all the equipment in another room. Everything was wired. It was really very professionally set up, to have it under totally controlled conditions.'

The main thrust of the work took place over five weeks up to Christmas 1972. It was an especially frantic time in modern American history; President Nixon had just been re-elected, the Watergate scandal was starting to come to light, the Vietnam war was reaching its crescendo, the USSR was clamping down on dissidents, and US airlines had started screening passengers for the first time to stave off a glut of hijackings.

The release of the Puthoff and Targ investigation's findings unfolded in parts. Before the work was finished, a constantly inquiring media was forewarned that something remarkable was up at Menlo Park.

Accordingly, like the opening scene of a movie, a dramatic holding statement went out in print and on TV from the head of SRI in 1973 saying, 'We have observed certain phenomena for which we have no scientific explanation.' It was a gift to the news media, and they gave the story extraordinary prominence. (SRI showed little sign of being media-shy at this exciting time for them. In 2011, a resident of Palo Alto, close to SRI, turned up a 23-centimetre-thick scrapbook clearly complied by the Institute, filled with hundreds of press cuttings on the Geller story from all over the world. The scrapbook seems to have ended up being thrown out with the garbage at some point, but is now in Uri's possession.)

Late in 1974, with the cream of the SRI work having appeared in *Nature,* a more wide-ranging analysis of the things Geller did at the Institute was released in a film made there, *Experiments With Uri Geller*, which Puthoff and Targ explained was made to 'share with the viewer observations of phenomena that in our estimation clearly deserve further study'. More observations, meanwhile, which Puthoff and Targ deemed too anecdotal for the film – or were noted informally without the cameras running – are still emerging 40 years on, as the two physicists and other major players like Kit Green reveal them.

The findings reported in the magazine concerned telepathy only, not metal bending. All the same, the material was so revolutionary for conservative science that the ripples it caused would be far-reaching. *Nature*'s editors warned in their preamble to the article that it was 'bound to create a stir in the scientific community', and added that the paper would be 'greeted with a preconditioned reaction amongst many scientists. To some, it simply confirms what they have always known or believed. To others, it is beyond the laws of science, and therefore necessarily unacceptable.'

Puthoff's and Targ's first conclusion was that Geller had succeeded in reproducing randomly chosen drawings made by people unknown to him, while he was in a double-walled steel room which was acoustically, visually and electrically shielded. The chance of him doing as well as he did by chance was calculated at a million to one.

In another test, where he was asked to 'guess' the face of a die shaken in a closed steel box – so the investigator could not possibly know the position of the die either – Geller managed the correct answer eight times out of ten. What was especially interesting was that the twice he did not get the answer, he had not attempted one, saying his perception was not clear. The die test, again, represented a million-to-one chance.

The rest of the *Nature* report concerned another psychic called Pat Price, a former California police commissioner. Price was a 'remote viewer', and in perceiving and describing in detail randomly chosen outdoor scenes from many kilometres away, he managed to beat odds of a billion to one. A third test on six unnamed psychics to see if their brainwaves could be measured responding to a flashing light in a distant room yielded one of the six with a measurable reaction in his brain.

Targ and Puthoff also speculated that 'remote perceptual ability' might be available to many of us, but we are unaware of it. They made the point that, although they had seen Uri bend metal in the laboratory, they had been unable to do a full, controlled experiment to support a paranormal hypothesis of metal bending.

The SRI Geller film went much further than the drier official report. Geller was first shown 'sending' numbers to Puthoff, Targ and Franklin, along with Don Scheuch, Vice President of Research at SRI. Then we see him playing what the experimenters call 'ten can Russian roulette', in which he successfully finds a steel ball in one of ten cans without touching them. He graduates from first doing this by holding his hands over the cans, to later detecting which one contains the ball as he walks into a room and sees them lined up on a blackboard sill. He also succeeds at the same test when one of the cans contains room-temperature water. When faced with a line-up of cans where one contains a sugar cube, or a paper-wrapped ball bearing, he passes and says he cannot be sure. We are told in the film that, whereas 'officially' SRI could only report Geller as having achieved a one-in-a million chance, in reality, and taking all the tests into account, he had defeated odds of a trillion to one against correctly guessing the cans' contents.

In the area of PK (psychokinesis, affecting materials with the power of the mind) which the experimenters did not touch in the *Nature* article, the film showed Geller decreasing and increasing the weight of a one-gram piece of metal on an electronic scale which has been covered by a bell jar; all Puthoff and Targ's precautions to preclude fraud by such methods as tapping the bell jar or even jumping on the floor are shown.

In another PK test, Geller successfully deflects a magnetometer to full scale, having first been checked out with the same instrument for magnets concealed on him. In another test, he is seen deflecting a compass needle, although the experimenters make the point that they are not satisfied by this test, not because they have any evidence of Uri cheating, but because they discover that a small, concealed piece of metal can in some circumstances produce the same effect. On spoon bending, the commentary was cautious, as it was on some tests the scientists had done on Uri's ability to bend rings. For these experiments, SRI had manufactured rings that required 68 kilograms of force to distort them; they did end up bent, but the laboratory had no film or experimental findings to confirm how they became so.

But many infinitely stranger things were happening around Uri in the PK arena, and although they were not made public or even formally reported as scientific findings, all were being reported informally back to CIA through Kit Green – who, with his own uncanny experiences to go on – was able to report ever more confidently to his bosses that Uri Geller was, as they had hoped, potentially a very potent weapon indeed.

As Hal Puthoff was to say, 'I feel it has been a privilege to have been exposed to 21st-century physics ahead of time.'

Others who reported strange events included the SRI film cameraman, an ex-*Life Magazine* war photographer, Zev Pressman, who was interviewed by the author in his 80s at his home in Palo Alto. Pressman said he had seen spoons bend 'dozens of times', and had both witnessed and videotaped an SRI stopwatch apparently materializing in midair from Hal Puthoff's briefcase, before dematerializing, then materializing again, and dropping down gently onto a table. SRI was too unsure about the segment being a Geller-inspired hoax to include it in its film.

Another day, Uri was having lunch in the SRI canteen with Russell Targ and lunar astronaut Edgar Mitchell. They had been talking about Mitchell's walk on the Moon the previous year, and about teleportation. Uri had ordered ice cream. In the first spoonful, he bit hard on something metallic. He spat it out to find a tiny arrowhead, which Mitchell looked at and exclaimed, 'My God! That looks familiar.' Back in the laboratory, the three were talking when they saw another small piece of metal fall to the carpet. When they picked it up, they saw that together, the two pieces made up a tiepin. According to Geller and Targ, Mitchell looked shocked. When asked why, he said he now realized why the first piece had looks so familiar. It was a tiepin he had lost several years before.

Targ was the more interested of the two lead scientists in the paranormal, but at the same time the more knowledgeable about magicians. On one occasion be endeavoured to try to blindside Geller by observing in an informal setting how he handled a pack of cards, certain that he would spot certain telltale signs of a professional.

'We were sitting round the table chatting,' says Puthoff, 'and Russ takes some cards, rips open the cellophane, and says, "Uri, do you ever do anything with cards?" and hands him the deck. Uri says, "No, I'm not into cards," and he reaches out to take the deck and clumsily drops part of it. Now our observation was that the cards appeared to fall and land and go partially *into* the table and fall over, so what we ended up with was several cards whose corners were cut off where they had appeared to go into the table. A whole piece of the card was missing. In the deck, of course, the cards were in order, and we had a certain place where they began to be slightly chopped, and the next one was a little more chopped and so on, from ten per cent of a card up to 30 or 40 per cent. There were about six or seven cards with part missing, and they were the ones that gave the impression of having dug into the table. It was very startling.

'Russ scooped up the cards immediately. The question was how did that happen. Without a doubt, there was no chance for Geller to substitute cards or to distract us while he cut pieces off. This was a one-second event. The only thing we could figure, since we weren't yet ready to believe that something so magical had happened, was that when the cards went through the machine in the factory, a certain set went through at an angle and got cut.

'So Russ checked with the card company, and asked if they ever had runs in which some of the cards get chopped. They said never, they had all sorts of procedures to prevent it, and it would be detected if it had occurred. Even on that basis, you have to say that the synchronicity that one of the few decks that ever got chopped should ever end up in Uri Geller's hand is unbelievable. But that's the kind of thing that happened around him.

'Another thing that happened was when everybody was over at our house for dinner, and my wife had made some mayonnaise, and set the spoon in the sink. We ate, and later when she went back, that spoon was all curled up but the mayonnaise on it had not been touched. It's hard to believe that it could've been done. Uri would have had to go in there, bend the spoon, then go the refrigerator, find more mayonnaise, swill it around, make sure it had untouched mayonnaise on it, and put it back in the sink. And we always watched him like a hawk. We always traded off that if one if us went to the bathroom, the other would watch him. Even in informal situations, myself, Russell, my wife, other friends we had over, I gave them all tasks: you concentrate on spoons, don't let them out of your sight; you concentrate on when he does drawings.

'Back at SRI, we were going to have Uri attempt to deflect a laser beam. This was a complex experiment, and he said, "How will I know if I am successful?" We said, "You see this chart recorder over here. That line is a recording of the position of the laser beam that is picked up and if you deflect the laser beam it will show as a signal on the chart." He said, "So what you want to see is a signal on this chart recorder. OK! One! Two! Three Go!" And the chart recorder went off scale, came back and was burned out.

'We took it to the repair shop and some of the electronics had been blown out. OK, so it could have been a coincidence, or our paranoid theory could have been correct, that he had some EMP pulse generator buried in his body somewhere and he stepped on a heel switch and made it blow.' Puthoff has no idea to this day. 'But,' he says, 'I have no doubt that he has genuine powers in the psi area.'

Still stranger things were going on at the DIA (Defense Intelligence Agency) in the wake of the Geller research at SRI, according to Eldon Byrd, a lieutenant commander in the US Navy Reserve, who had left the full-time military to work as a civilian strategic-weapons systems expert at the Naval Surface Weapons Center in Washington DC.

With top-level secret security clearance, and contacts high in the CIA and DIA, Byrd was interested in non-lethal weaponry, especially biological warfare when used humanely to infect an enemy with *reversible* illness. To further his knowledge, he went back to school and in 1970, got a PhD in medical engineering, at George Washington University. He would later get involved in still more rarefied areas of defence, such as using electromagnetics as a weapon to confuse people, as a reversible process, and in experiments on thought transference.

It was only when Byrd, who the author interviewed before he died in 2002, started investigating Uri Geller and the whole psychic and remote-viewing arena, that he found himself in an area classified as beyond top secret and presented with a confidentiality document he had never seen before. 'The amusing thing about this document was there were twelve items on it saying I wouldn't do this and that, and the last item said, by signing this document, I agreed that the government would deny that I ever signed the document,' he recalled.

The reason for such paranoia, it turned out, was that one aspect of the most secret work Puthoff and Targ were doing (and still don't discuss) was even more challenging to science than remote viewing.

'They had a situation,' Byrd explained, 'where they had the remote viewer in some location covered by a satellite going over and taking pictures so they could tell whether the remote viewer's data was correct. So the viewer drew a map of a compound at a location and there was a tank here and a building over here and when they got the photo back to compare there were some things he said were there that weren't on the photograph. That is, until two years later. That was what really got them going, *precognitive* remote viewing.'

To check out further whether this could really be the case, in 1974 when the eerie future-predicting viewing seemed to be occurring, they developed a way of ensuring completely random locations for the remote viewer to try to envision.

'The idea was for Puthoff, in a particular instance I knew of, not to know himself where he was heading. So Hal would drive along and if a car got behind them, they would slow down and let the car pass them. If the letter R or a couple of others appeared on the licence plate, they would turn right at the next intersection. Anything else, they would turn left, so they just randomly generated a location and when they got there, 30 minutes later they would take pictures and bring them back. So back at SRI, they would see there's the Chinese restaurant and Hal standing with his foot up with a blue jacket on and the marina and so on.

'But when they got back and listened to the tape of the remote viewer, it was mind-boggling. He was seeing what was going to happen half an hour before it did happen. One of the physicists, a friend of mine, said this is the most important thing we had discovered, and this was why we were ahead of the Soviets, because they can't believe in such phenomena because to them, precognitive remote viewing, precognitive anything, can't exist. The future hasn't happened yet. It cannot be determined. The future can only be in the mind of God and there is no God.'

Kit Green, meanwhile, whose similarity (in function if not form) to the sceptical fictional Agent Dana Scully of the X-Files, was soon to find himself at the centre of something still stranger involving Geller, this at one of the most secret defence facilities in the USA, the super-secure nuclear research and development centre, Lawrence Livermore National Laboratory, an hour or so northeast of SRI.

By 1974, a few staff at Livermore, a former Naval base, had become concerned that if Uri Geller was genuine, he was potentially a danger to national security. It didn't take more than the movement of a few grams of nuclear material a few centimetres, after all, to set off (or sabotage) a nuclear weapon. Although the world knew by this time that Geller was being tested at SRI, and a select few knew the work was government-funded, it would still have been considered a step too bizarre (not to mention dangerous) for the Livermore Laboratory to do any official work on Geller.

Between scientific engagements, after all, Uri was fast becoming a showbiz animal, hopping from talk show to celebrity party to talk show. To be investigating him formally would just not have been appropriate. So a small, volunteer group of physicists and engineers at Livermore, with Green's knowledge, embarked on a series of experiments with Geller on evenings and at weekends, in an old, wooden barracks on a low-security part of the former naval air base.

The tests were designed to succeed in the PK area where SRI had, in formal testing at least, failed. As experiments, again, they fell frustratingly short. Geller could do everything he was asked in the way of metal bending, and also in wiping computer floppy disks, a talent which, as we will see, would be employed by the CIA when they began to use him for actual operations. But, crucially, he could still only get a reliable hit rate when he was allowed to touch the items he was working on. An extraordinary psychological backdrop unfolded, however, among the six volunteer researchers, which would unquestionably have had Scully and Mulder arguing and speculating through an entire episode. The events were first detailed in a fine 1997 book, *Remote Viewers*, by the author Jim Schnabel, who has written for *Nature*, *Science*, *New Scientist*, the *Washington Post*, *The Guardian* and *The Independent*. However, Schnabel was only able to identify Green (Geller's 'Rick') as 'Richard Kennett' whereas now Dr Green is able to confirm all the events as accurate in his own name.

What was to become a mounting hysteria, practically a mass-possession, began when one of the group, a security officer, Ron Robertson, was speaking on the phone to Geller, and Geller proceeded in mid-conversation, his voice having oddly changed and gone up an octave, to give him a detailed prediction of three family dramas, all of which happened to the officer the following Saturday. Then, in the makeshift lab, an infrared camera started recording unexplained patches of radiation high up on a wall. Kodak, the film manufacturer, was discreetly asked to examine the results. The company could not even begin to explain them. Shortly afterwards, a tape recorder picked up a peculiar, unintelligible metallic voice, a voice no one had heard when the machine was on. When Green later examined the metallic voice tape, one of the few recognizable words on it was the codename for an unconnected top-secret project, which he happened to know about, but nobody at Livermore could have any inkling of.

As Uri became an occasional fixture around the laboratory, some members of the team and their families began to see fuzzy, grey 3D hallucinations or visions, or something, of miniature, comic book-style flying saucers hovering in the centre of various rooms. Other visions the scientists reported, in mounting terror, took the form of giant birds, which would walk across their gardens, or, in the case of one physicist, Mike Russo, and his wife, the foot of their bed.

After a few weeks, another physicist, Peter Crane, called Dr Green at CIA, almost in desperation. Green came down and met Crane in a coffee shop in Livermore town, near the lab. He later met the other team members, and was astonished to find them sweating and weeping openly as they described what had been happening. Decades later, as a medical doctor, Green was still pondering the implications of this apparent assault on the team's state of mind.

Knowing that group hallucinations are extremely rare, and additionally, that all the affected Livermore personnel, as a part of their high security clearance, were known to be unusually stable psychologically, Green doubted the hallucination theory even more. 'I was confident at the time, as I am now, that there was no psychiatric pathology,' Dr Green says today of these almost extravagantly weird events of 40 years ago. 'I realized quickly that it had none of the signs of mass hysteria. There was no endogenous psychopathology on behalf of the individuals there. They were not psychiatrically ill. But that doesn't mean they didn't get scared to death.'

You can see why, when it turns out that Russo, after telling Green what had been happening, then received a phone call from the metallic voice, insisting that the Livermore group cease its work on Geller – something the scientists, who were only volunteers after all, did with some alacrity, and whereupon the phenomena gradually stopped.

One of the last but most extreme of the phenomena appeared to a physicist called Don Curtis and his wife. It consisted of a holographic false arm in grey suiting material and was hovering in their living room then rotating like it was on a spit. The arm had no hand, but a hook. Hearing about this vision-too-far prompted Green to return to California and ask Puthoff and Targ for an urgent meeting. He even wondered privately if the SRI men, both laser physicists, were playing some kind of holography prank on their scientific colleagues at a rival lab, and he wanted them to know the joke had gone far enough.

Late at night, in Green's motel room in Livermore, Targ And Puthoff, who were colleagues and friends of the CIA man, turned up. He started telling the SRI scientists, having by now clinically evaluated the affected scientists, the full, bizarre story of what he had been told was happening at the laboratory, ending on the *pièce de résistance*, the arm apparition, and hoping to extract a confession and draw a line under the crazy business.

'I was demonstrably angry. I was demonstrably upset and I raised my voice, and it was at the absolute instant when I told them about the holographic arm scenario, when I was pounding the tabletop, asking them what in the living hell was going on and saying, "What exactly do you guys know about this absolute bizarre nonsense?" It was at that exact millisecond that an aggressive banging started on the room door and scared the living hell out of us. It was like somebody was trying to break down the door.'

By now, according to Puthoff, he and Targ suspected Green might now be the playing a practical joke on them. The CIA man answered the door to reveal a middle-aged man in a grey suit, who wandered stiffly into the room, stood between the beds and said in an odd, slow voice, 'I guess I must be in the wrong room,' before walking slowly out again. All three men noticed as he left that one sleeve of his suit was empty.

'This diminutive, relatively short and taciturn, relatively grey man, grey in both his ashen appearance and his suit wasn't stomping or screaming when he walked into the room. He was just gently walking, slowly and carefully, after pounding on the door like that. And he said what he said, walked out, when we saw the pinned-up arm of his suit. After five or ten seconds, we tore out of the room one, one way, one, the other, one down the stairwell, but he was gone. None of us felt that it was an apparition or some shape-shifting, ghost-like cloud figure. It looked like an absolutely everyday ordinary human being with nothing odd about it except the missing arm pinned up in its grey suit sleeve. It was as real as it gets.'

Not for the first time as Dr Green relates this story in 2013, you have to remind yourself that it is not being told by a horror author or a credulous paranormal junkie – or, indeed, by Uri Geller – but by a former CIA scientist, now a distinguished professor of medicine in his 70s at the biggest medical school in the USA.

So how did the three scientists confronted with this event in the motel room in Livermore react immediately after it happened? 'Our discussion was a little more mundane after the event than you might expect,' says Green, 'because we had been working together for a long time and regarding the

Dr. Kit Green, former CIA Assistant National Intelligence Officer.

matter of paranormal activity existing, well, we were already beyond that. We had already gotten to the point that scientists do where you make an observation in the laboratory that you don't understand and you know you've got to collect more data, but you know it's not magic and it's not a gremlin. You don't know what it is, and in the case of this kind of work it was an extension of a sort of paranormal landscape, none of which we really understood at that time. We understand it better today, but we still don't understand most of it.

'So we knew we didn't have a physics that would explain what we were seeing, both at Livermore and SRI and the motel room, and dozens of other circumstances in which absolutely clearly odd but veridical – that's to say is very true – data was being acquired which showed that Uri and other individuals were producing information that could only otherwise be obtained by satellites. There was nothing that could be tampered with, so there was no concern in our minds that this was a magic show.

'Where there was concern in our minds was, what did we think the chances were that somebody had a listening device in our room – that someone was running an operation to test our gullibility? We discussed not whether it was a magic trick, but was it a national entity of some sort was doing this. We talked extensively about how somebody – yes, maybe the KGB – could have arranged to have someone listening, and at the moment when I was asking about the severed arm scenario, bang on the door and do something that would fit the story I was telling.

'It takes some believing that it was the KGB. And I didn't really worry that it was the United States government doing it because they knew by then, after a number of years, that the phenomenology was absolutely real because we were testing it in circumstances where the controls were architected to be absolutely foolproof. And the events couldn't possibly be magician controlled because it was orders of magnitude more complicated than magicians could achieve. So we knew the government knew this was real, so it wasn't our government trying to destabilize us.'

The strange Livermore events are unique in the Uri Geller story in that they are the only instance to be found of anything that might be described as a dark happening around him, the stuff indeed of witchdoctors, black magic and nightmares. Nowhere else is there a report, however fanciful, of such things happening, let alone a group of nuclear scientists becoming unhinged because of seemingly paranormal experiences. Uri and other serious people who know him well have pondered over the years on whether his subconscious, objected to him working with men whose job was researching and developing nuclear warheads. It seems odd that something so frightening to others would happen just this once, when he happened to be working with people who helped create weapons capable of wiping out most of the world.

'The effect on the scientists was life changing, so it seems. To my knowledge, they all, or most of them, resigned,' says Kit Green. 'I don't know the details, but the information I had was that they quit from Livermore. The reason I had been meeting with them, after all, was that they wanted to quit.'

* * *

Uri's life as the subject of scientific experimentation in the early 1970s continued in so many laboratories that he sometimes struggles to remember which was which. The weirdness that surrounded him wherever he went continued too; the very profusion of strange events affecting hundreds of people would suggest that, were he a uniquely talented trickster, he would still, as Kit Green argues, have needed the backroom staff of 50 David Copperfields (or half the KGB's manpower) to arrange for dazzling, puzzling, seemingly inexplicable and inexorable happenings to shoot off in their hundreds and thousands like a years-long fireworks display.

When, some while after the SRI programme ended, the US Army centralized all the psychic research being done around the country into one overarching military psychic project based at Fort George G. Meade US Army post in Maryland, home of the National Security Agency and the Defense Information Systems Agency, Uri was not on the psychics roster for some reason.

Could this be because he was seen as having powers greater than other high-quality psychics such as former police commissioner, Pat Price, and was part of a greater plan altogether? Was it because Uri was becoming paranoid that the Russians, the Arabs, or even his patrons at the CIA would attempt to assassinate him? Was it because, as Puthoff and Targ now maintain, spectacular and baffling though his abilities were, in terms of reliability he wasn't actually the best of the psychics the US government had to hand? Was it because his devotion to the American cause was diluted by his loyalty to Israel? The two countries are longstanding allies, but this doesn't mean Israeli intelligence doesn't spy on the USA and the USA on Israel; this is the way of the real world.

In terms of loyalty to US interests, Uri had to be regarded by anyone sensible as a young, green, very slightly loose cannon at the very least; apart from anything else, he was still a foreign national, living in the USA on a visa. Or was Uri's withdrawal from lab experimentation simply a matter of a young, handsome, single man being bored and wanting to get on with being, as one of his best American friends of the time puts it, 'a freakin' rock star'?

Dr David Morehouse, a career army man recruited into the Fort Meade programme as a remote viewer, but who was also given the privilege of overviewing the programme to a certain extent, maintains that Uri was the most remarkable of the psychics available.

'I came to know of Uri when I was in the remote-viewing unit because one of the first things you were required to do was go through the historical files, and in these files were constant references to Uri and Uri's early involvement at Stanford Research Institute,' Morehouse says. 'It was very clear in all of the historical documentation, the briefs that were passed on to the intelligence community, that Uri Geller was without equal. None of the others came even close to Uri's abilities in all of the tests.

'What interested me was that this was not a phenomenon that was born in some back room behind a beaded curtain by a starry-eyed guy; this was something that was born in a bed of science at Stanford Research Institute, being paid for heavily by the CIA. And also, these were two laser physicists, not psychologists, but hard scientists brought in to establish the validity and credibility, to see if it works as an intelligence collection asset, and if it works, to develop training templates that allow us to select certain individuals that meet a certain psychological profile, and establish units that can gather and collect data using certain phenomenon. And their answer to all those things was 'Yes'. If Targ and Puthoff had said, "Well, yes, there is a little something to it, but we can't explain it, it's not consistent and isn't of any value," well fine, but obviously it met all the criteria and 20-odd years later, they were still using it.'

But the testing took its toll on Uri. When celebrities are interviewed by the media, they often get frustrated at being asked the same questions a thousand times, and wonder why each journalist feels the need to start every interview with, 'So when were you born?' or something equally basic. Scientists are similar; each programme of experimentation started from the very beginning, with the boring basics – boring at least to those who have been through the process many times.

When you think that Uri was probably unique in the whole history of celebrity in that he was simultaneously going through the chat-show interview mill *and* intensive and repetitive scientific investigation, it is a wonder he didn't crack up. The amount of time he spent wired up in laboratories in the early 1970s is astonishing. On top of SRI's work and that of Eldon Byrd, something we will read more of in the next chapter, he was investigated formally by several more laboratories, and did countless informal demonstrations to interested scientists.

In the United States, Uri did laboratory work with Dr Franklin at Kent State University – research that led to Franklin's report, *Fracture surface physics indicating teleneural interaction*. He also worked with Dr Thelma Moss of the Neuropsychiatric Institute at UCLA's Center for the Health Sciences, Dr Coohill at Western Kentucky University, and with William E. Cox at The Institute of Parapsychology at Durham, North Carolina. In Europe, he underwent testing at Birkbeck College and King's College, both parts of London University, and at France's INSERM Telemetry Laboratories, part of the Foch Hospital in Suresnes. In South Africa, he was examined by Dr E. Alan Price, a medical doctor and Research Project Director for the South African Institute for Parapsychology, who painstakingly documented over 100 cases of Geller's effect on members of the public and university staffs as he travelled across South Africa on a lecture tour.

The reaction of scientists who met him informally, meanwhile, was almost routinely startling. The MIT (Massachusetts Institute of Technology) professor Victor Weisskopf, who had worked with the quantum pioneers Werner Heisenberg, Erwin Schrödinger, Wolfgang Pauli and Niels Bohr, and was on the Manhattan Project that developed the atomic bomb, said, 'I was shocked and amazed [at] how Mr Geller bent my office key at MIT while I was holding it.

The sturdy key kept bending in my hand. I cannot explain this phenomenon. I can only assume that it could relate to quantum chromodynamics' [a specialized area of quantum related to String Theory].

Professor George Pake, a member of the president's Science Advisory Committee and creator of Xerox's Palo Alto Research Centre (Parc) said, 'During our conversation, he demonstrated his mind-reading techniques and plucked out of my mind an image I was thinking of. It was very impressive.'

Over in the UK, the prominent Oxford neuropsychiatrist, Dr Peter Fenwick, spoke at length about Uri. 'I was able to

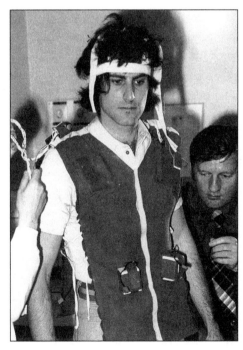

Uri being tested at an INSERM laboratory in France.

watch him bend a spoon on a colleague's outstretched hand. I took a spoon from the table. Uri did not touch it. I put it on my colleague's hand and asked Uri to bend it. Uri ran his finger above the spoon and stood back. Nothing happened. We expressed some disappointment, still watching the spoon. He said, "Wait and watch." Slowly, as we watched, with Uri standing well away, the spoon started to curl in front of us, and within four minutes the tail of the spoon had risen up like a scorpion's sting. I then took the spoon, the first time I had handled it since I put it there, and sure enough, it remained a normal spoon with a marked bend.'

Dr Wernher von Braun, the NASA scientist and father of the US space programme, met Uri and announced: 'Geller has bent my ring in the palm of my hand without ever touching it. Personally, I have no scientific explanation for the phenomena.' The MIT physics professor Gerald Schroeder, latterly of the Weizmann Institute of Science in Israel, had a different slant on the Geller enigma. 'What makes me accept Geller at face value,' he said, 'is that unlike a magician, he does not have a bag of tricks. He bends spoons. The one he bent with me peering over his shoulder continued to bend even after he placed it on the ground and stepped away. The Talmud claims there are two types of "magic". One is the "catching of the eye", an optical illusion. The other is the real thing, a mustering of the forces of nature. With Uri, I opt for the latter, though he claims he has no idea how these are mustered.'

But after all, perhaps it is possible, even for someone desperately anxious to be taken seriously by science, to become worn out by being a lab rat. 'The government saw that they couldn't really control me,' Uri Geller says, 'because

Uri with Edgar Mitchell (*far right*) and Wernher von Braun at NASA's Goddard Space Flight Center, after bending von Braun's wedding ring in the palm of the scientist's hand. Picture taken with German Minox spy camera by Shipi.

I was really on an ego trip and into making money and into show business. I didn't want to sit in a laboratory any more, doing the same thing again and again, without getting paid, and then getting constantly abused in the background by the sceptics with their silly, far-fetched explanations of what I did. Some of these people were really low – ignorant and lying, like medieval witch finders.'

All in all, he felt – and indeed knew – that his abilities were accepted beyond serious question by the US government, right to the top. Yet although Uri's period as an experimental subject was drawing to an end, his life as an American spy was just about to begin.

Chapter Three

A SUBJECT OF INTEREST

The path which led Uri Geller from playground prodigy in the back streets of Tel Aviv – a story we will recount later – to young man groomed as the public face of a US government programme designed, essentially, to create a team of psychic spies working against the 'evil empire' of the Soviet bloc, starts in earnest in Cyprus in the late 1950s. Uri and his mother had moved to the island to live with his new stepfather, Ladislas Gero, who ran a modest motel in Nicosia. Gero died a year after the move, leaving Uri's mother alone again – but in Cyprus, with Uri newly settled in as a boarder at the prestigious Terra Santa Catholic School in the hills outside the city.

Uri, a notably imaginative little boy, had, with the unusual powers he seemed to have acquired, long dreamed of putting his abilities to use as a spy or special agent of some kind. The primacy of intelligence in the espionage sense is close to a founding virtue of the state of Israel and has been key to the country's survival against the odds in modern times.

One of the most common symbols seen in Israel, used on everything from food labels to official literature, shows two men carrying a huge bunch of grapes. It is known to every Israeli schoolchild that these men were two of a group of 12 spies, sent by Moses to check out whether the land of milk and honey promised by God really was as fertile as He had told Moses it would be. The grapes were the evidence they brought back to show it very much was the Promised Land that had been yearned for since Abraham's day.

In 1959, Uri was a 13-year-old, tearing around Nicosia on his bicycle like many other youngsters. As we will see, he was known to some boys and teachers at Terra Santa to have some very odd abilities, but it seems like any child striving to appear normal and unexceptional, he kept his paranormal powers mostly under wraps. He told no one about what he called a green television screen he could envisage.

His stepfather's unprepossessing little motel happened to be close to the Israeli consulate, and attracted a few business visitors from Israel. One of them was Yoav Shacham, a tall, well-built man in the grain-buying business. Uri was a sociable lad who missed his father, a career soldier back in Israel, and became friendly with the tough-looking Shacham. He reminded Uri of his father: certainly not his stepfather, who had been a gentle, mild, older man. Uri, who went by the more Greek name of George, now mostly spoke English but enjoyed speaking Hebrew with this interesting man, who knew judo and offered to teach him some moves. But while they were practising, Uri says he got the feeling that Shacham was somehow more than a grain buyer. He saw that Shacham got mail from Arab countries, and moreover, Uri believed he could see on his mental TV screen that his friend was both adept with firearms and working with secret documents in some way. It occurred to the young teenager that Shacham was a spy, something that appealed intensely to his increasingly cinema-fired imagination.

One afternoon, Uri says, that when he had to go into the motel's loft, he found himself above Shacham's room, from where he could hear a conversation, one which seem to have clear espionage overtones. Peering through a crack around the ceiling light, Uri saw his friend with someone who looked to be a middle-aged Egyptian, who he gathered from what was being said, appeared to live in Israel. The two were poring over documents, which they were photographing and which Uri could see were in Arabic. The men were speaking quietly about the Egyptian Army, something happening in the Sudan and some business concerning agricultural machinery among other matters.

Uri was thrilled and excited. Yoav must be a real Mossad agent! It was the stuff his dreams were made of come true. 'I wanted to share the secret of the powers with someone I didn't know too well,' he explained years later. When Uri told Shacham what he suspected, the agent, as might be expected, was horrified, and probably more than a little ashamed that he had failed so amateurishly to cover his tracks. He confirmed that Uri was correct, and appealed to his young countryman's patriotism to keep it to himself. Heaven knows what Shacham thought when the boy to whom he had just been obliged to entrust his deadly important secret told him he was the possessor of inexplicable, magical powers.

Uri asked him to think of numbers, which he guessed correctly each time. He made Shacham's watch hands move. When Shacham invited him out for a walk, Uri told him as they strolled through the streets that he would do anything to spy for Israel, too. Shacham said that he was far too young, but then truly put his life in Uri's hands when he went on, 'But you can help me.' This was the start of a routine whereby, whenever Shacham was away from Cyprus, Uri would collect his mail at the motel and deliver it on his bike directly to the Israeli consul, a one-armed, red-haired man in his 40s. His loyalty was such that he told none of his friends, not even his mother, what he was doing. But he did make one possible mistake for a spy when he wore on first mission to the consulate an Israeli insignia that his father had won.

The consul zoomed in on it, asking gently whose it was. Uri proudly told him about his father being a sergeant

Uri, aged 11, with his father, Tibor.

major in the Tank Corps. The consul smoothly extracted every detail from Uri. Later, back in Israel, his father came home to find his apartment had been almost taken apart by intruders, although nothing had been stolen. Yoav and Uri, his unpaid courier, meanwhile became close friends. Uri met Yoav's fiancée, Tammi, and he promised Uri that when he had finished his military duty at 21, he would gladly help the young man get into the secret service. He was quite specific about what the boy should do when he was eventually conscripted, instructing him to join the Paras, get himself into officer school – 'And then find me.'

When the time came, Uri knew he had to shine in his army career before the Mossad would even consider him. He served well and loyally for the most part and became a paratrooper as Yoav had directed. He even saw his friend once in the front of a Jeep – the Mossad man seemed to have returned to his own paratroop unit – and, delighted, said hello to him. Uri, who was later wounded while serving in the Six Day War, eventually got into officer school. But as it turned out, the Israeli Defense Forces and Uri Geller were not quite made for one another. While Uri was on his officer-training course, he read in a newspaper that Yoav Shacham had been killed in action. His desire for a military career took an instant nosedive. That very night while on an exercise he fell asleep on duty and had to kicked awake by an officer. His days on the training course came to an end shortly afterwards.

'Yoav was the key to the door for my future,' Uri says. 'His death sank me into despair, firstly because I loved and cared for him, and then because I knew my career was down the drain. Only he really knew of my powers. Suddenly, officer school didn't seem so important and I was quickly thrown

Yoav Shacham, the Mossad agent who recruited 16-year-old Uri as an unpaid, bicycle-riding courier in Cyprus. Yoav is with his fiancée Tammi and Uri's mother.

out. My father, who was devastated, advised me to try again. He had been a sergeant major and was desperate for me to do better than he had and make it to officer rank. But for me, leaving and going back to my unit was a great relief. A big responsibility was lifted, and I felt fine about it.'

Yet while he kept his paranormal abilities largely quiet in the military, rumours about his remarkable abilities still got around, especially towards the end of his three-year mandatory service period, at the end of 1968. After being wounded in the Six Day War, he had been given the rather pleasant and easy army job of running around Israel on a Vespa scooter he had brought back from Cyprus, tracking down deserters – something he was, unsurprisingly perhaps, very good at. It was about this time, while still in uniform, that he began showing more colleagues what he could do, and was invited by pals to perform at youth clubs and parties.

After returning to civilian life, broke but happy, with his scooter and with a beautiful young model girlfriend in tow, he became a male model, gracing magazine advertisements in some natty swimwear or smart Terylene jackets. While he was on shoots, he would do impromptu demonstrations of his powers for the photographers and technicians, and he began to be invited – for payment – to perform at 'arty' parties. Uri, loving fame more and more, was beginning a determined clamber up Israel's social ladder. Soon, as word

Uri had a brief career as a male model. He is seen here in a stylish tailored Terylene mod jacket.

got out about a Six Day War veteran, now a male model, who could perform incomprehensible psychic feats, his audiences began to include lawyers, politicians – and senior military officers. Before long, he was being approached by someone he believed to be a Mossad agent, who invited him to do a show at a military base of some kind.

He found himself being taken to a place called Midrasha. 'It's just out of Tel Aviv, near Herzliya,' he says, 'on a hill and it's top secret. You know … it's all cameras everywhere and barbed wire. They were all Mossad and Secret Service agents, and generals, and spies, and you name it. And I was taken there to give a big lecture, and I think I blew their minds. I moved the hands of a watch. I did mind reading. I instilled pictures in other people's minds. I did things that they could grab and twist for their own missions.'

He began, in tandem with his show business work in Israel – which was making him one of the most famous men in the country – to undertake operational missions for the secret service. Aharon Yariv, head of military intelligence, met him in a coffee shop to discuss how he might help. Meir Amit, the head of the Mossad, was a powerful supporter of Geller and believer in his powers. Although he resigned in 1968, he remained close to the organization and continued to advocate deploying Uri on a range of tasks. Uri still refuses to reveal specific jobs he was assigned, but he became known by all the major establishment figures of the time, especially the defence minister and military hero, Moshe Dayan, who specifically asked him if he could 'do certain things'.

'I answered to some yes, to some no. And then to the ones that I said yes to, he arranged for me to execute those requests, and those I cannot talk about. Not to be too specific, I think one of the interesting questions was whether my mind could knock out a pilot's mind in flight. Whether I could beam my powers and somehow mix up or jumble up a fighter pilot's mind.' The only actual task Uri speaks about from this time was successfully locating a piece of antique pottery for Dayan at an archaeological dig. Dayan would ask him to do the same again on other occasions, an offence under Israeli law, but not one he would be prosecuted for by anybody.

A variety of sources agree that the Israelis were intellectually open to the military and intelligence potential of Geller years before the USA, and the value Israel continues to place on Uri today cannot be underestimated. His work for the land of his birth is the area that he is the most reticent to discuss, perhaps because it is ongoing. The one thing he will say is that if he does anything for Israel, and he's not necessarily saying he does, 'it is only for totally positive causes'.

One slightly younger soldier whom Uri met when still in uniform and doing a performance is the current Israeli prime minister, Benjamin Netanyahu. The two remain close and see each other regularly. 'His abilities made a tremendous impression on me as a young soldier,' Netanyahu says today. 'I'm still amazed, I haven't a clue how he does these things.' And it is Netanyahu, listed 23rd on the 2012 *Forbes* magazine list of 'The World's Most Powerful People', who tells one of the more remarkable stories of Uri's metal-bending prowess. Netanyahu and his wife, Sara, were with Uri in a restaurant in Caesarea when Uri *simultaneously* bent the spoons of a whole group of people, all of whom were sitting at different tables – a rare example of a batch bending that caused astonishment in the restaurant.

Uri with Israeli Prime Minister Benjamin Netanyahu.

As we know from Kit Green's account in the previous chapter, back in the early 1970s, the Mossad was keen to swap intelligence with the USA, to the extent that it alerted the Americans to the unusual young man and told them that it was willing to allow the US intelligence and scientific communities to take a look at him. The Mossad's overture was followed by Andrija Puharich's mission to Israel to do semi-formal testing on Uri, and his eventual arrival in the USA in 1972.

During the two intense years that followed, the espionage world only touched Uri insofar as the circus that was going on around him. Mossad people were watching the SRI: CIA people were watching the SRI: and, according to a book on the Mossad written in 1978 by the well-informed writer

Richard Deacon, various Soviet-bloc spooks were watching them all. Uri had only a hazy knowledge of what was going on. He was not privy to the increasing interest being taken in him as a possible intelligence asset. As he says himself, he was becoming more and more interested in being a celebrity and making a lot of money.

* * *

The period when Uri Geller begins being used by the CIA – an unprecedented development since he was still an Israeli citizen – as well as by Mossad and the Mexican government – begins around 1974.

There was reluctance and caution at the CIA even then to exploit Geller. 'As we finished our work with Uri at SRI,' says the former astronaut Edgar Mitchell, 'I was called by the head of the CIA and asked to come to Washington and brief him on what we had learned. That head happened to be Ambassador George HW Bush' [who later, of course, became president]. Mitchell explained to Bush that the Russians were studying parapsychology, so it was essential that the CIA should be studying it, too. Geller was not immediately recruited as an agent, but Kit Green began regularly talking with Eldon Byrd about the Geller question.

Eldon Byrd, the naval strategic weapons systems specialist who had been one of many experts investigating Uri on behalf of the military, also briefed a CIA director, whom he didn't identify as Bush. 'In later years during the Brezhnev period,' he said before his death in 2002, 'I met with several Russian scientists who not only had documented results similar to ours, but also were actively using psychic techniques against the USA and its allies. I eventually ended up briefing a director of the CIA. I also briefed people on the National Security Council and I briefed Congressional committees because of some of the results we got.'

Byrd recalled getting a request from Green to come and see them. He again did not reveal Green's identity when interviewed. 'I went down to Virginia, and they said we understand you had an interaction with Uri a couple of years ago, and what did you do with him?' Byrd briefed Green and others at a meeting about some work he had done with Uri and a new, then secret, alloy of nickel and titanium called nitinol. Nitinol had a unique property of having a mechanical memory; it sprang back to the shape at which it was forged, whatever twisting and distortion it was subjected to. Byrd had given Uri a 12.5-centimetre-long piece of nitinol wire. Uri stroked it whereupon, according to Byrd, an odd little lump formed in it, which failed to disappear as it should have done. Bent nitinol, in Uri's hands, also refused to spring back into its original shape. In this and further tests with the alloy, Uri produced a molecular-level effect in it which, the lab reported, would have required Geller to have raised the temperature of the metal to almost 500°C.

Green's team at Langley was interested in this, as well they might be, but it was telepathy they seemed keener to discuss, and Byrd had some interesting experiences to relate. 'Uri had written something on a piece of paper, handed it to me and said, "Put this in your hand and don't look at it now. I'm going to think of a letter, and I want to see if you can pick it up." He closed his eyes, but nothing was happening in my head. So I thought, maybe I have to close my eyes for this to work. I closed them, and bam, there's a big green R lit up in my head. So I said, "I guess it's an R," and he said, "Yes, open the paper," and it was an R. When Byrd had got home that night, he reported to Green, he and his wife, Kathleen, were up until late transmitting increasingly complex pictures to one another flawlessly. 'I thought, man, somehow Uri tuned me up and I can even transfer the ability to my wife. But the next day, we tried again, and it wouldn't work.'

One of the areas the CIA, and soon the military too, was most interested in at this time was teaching people to develop their own telepathic – and possibly even psychokinetic – powers, so they were all ears at what Byrd had to say. 'I told him about the telepathy,' he recalled, 'and they said, "So you say it was a green R that came in your head?" I said, "Yes", and they looked at each other. I asked if there was something significant about the colour and they said there was.

'Another time,' Byrd continued, 'Uri asked me to check with my CIA guy, because he was living in the States and had the benefit of being here, and wanted to do something like work for the CIA on a project or something. So I passed that along to them and they said, "No! We won't do that". I said, "He's offering for free, why not?" They said that they had had bad experiences working with double agents. "So we don't do it." They told me that they knew he was working with the Mossad. I said he'd never told me he was working with the Mossad. There had been a couple of instances of requests, but that didn't mean working with or working for. "No!' they said. "We know he works with the Mossad."

'Later on, my contact person, who was head at the time of a division called Life Sciences [who we now know was Green] was regularly asking me if I knew where Uri was and what he was doing. Finally, I asked, "Why are you so curious?" They said they were assigned to keep track of him. I said this implies that you know he's for real. "Of course we know he's for real," they said, and went on to tell me that they'd tested him without his knowing who they were.' (This, of course, relates to the home experiment Green recounts in Chapter 1.)

Green told Byrd that he had seen a tape of Uri cheating, but it didn't make much difference, because they had seen him make spoons and forks bend on their own, so they were convinced that he was genuine. But this time, they were taping it under a certain set of protocols, and they said the proof to them that Uri was not a magician was that when they caught him cheating, the way he did it was so naïve that a magician wouldn't have thought he could get away with it.

The question of whether Uri has ever cheated or used a bit of sleight of hand, to please experimenters – or audiences – remains a tricky one. He vehemently denies it to this day, apart from one instance back in Israel, on which he is completely open. But there are those, including his most influential proponent, Green, who believe he may have enhanced his effects at times when his powers were at a low ebb, as they occasionally were. Many who know him have suggested that Uri does occasionally use a bit of sleight of hand. It seems to be something he does with no great skill to muddy the waters around him and create controversy. He appears to enjoy lowering people's expectations by doing a fairly obvious bit of routine magic – and then, when they have decided he's just a trickster, hitting them with something truly inexplicable. He even sometimes says he sees this as a safety mechanism. 'If you think about it, I probably would have been eliminated years ago if it was unanimously agreed that I was real,' he says.

(Green's opinion that when Uri did cheat, he did so, as others have noted, like a pretty hopeless amateur magician

– rather than the skilled one his detractors claim he is – is an interesting one. Remember Russell Targ's experience when he witnessed how Uri handled cards clumsily? Another view often proposed by students of Uri is that all sorts of professionals cut corners in various ways without negating the essential substance of their core ability. The Argentinian footballer Diego Maradona once scored a crucial goal against England by illegally touching the ball with his hand, and while it wasn't exactly a glorious episode in his career, nobody seriously says he is a fraud who can't play football at all; despite his obvious foul, he is commonly regarded as one of the most gifted players of all time. It might be added that the seven-times Tour de France winner Lance Armstrong was actually a pretty fine cyclist even without the performance-enhancing drugs that brought his career crashing down.)

Another figure on the American military/espionage landscape who was seriously assessing Uri Geller's warfare potential in the early 1970s was John B. Alexander, a special forces colonel engaged, as Eldon Byrd was for the Navy, in exploring on the US Army's behalf the paranormal's potential as a non-lethal military weapon. Alexander – who is widely (but incorrectly) regarded as the character played by George Clooney in *The Men Who Stare At Goats* had commanded undercover military teams in Vietnam and Thailand, and later moved into military science, working as Director of the Advanced Systems Concepts Office, US Army Laboratory Command, then Chief of Advanced Human Research with INSCOM, the intelligence and security command.

On retirement in 1988, Alexander joined Los Alamos National Laboratory with a brief to develop the concept of non-lethal defence. With his rare PhD in thanatology – the scientific study of death – he has strongly believed for a long while that inducing recoverable disease in an enemy's troops is preferable to blowing their bodies apart. He has written in this respect in several defence publications, including *Harvard International Review* and *Jane's International Defence Review*, and been written about in publications from *The Wall Street Journal* to *Scientific American*.

John Alexander now runs a privately funded science consultancy in Nevada, and he is a powerful advocate both of psychokinesis (PK) as a genuine phenomenon and of Geller as the possessor of PK abilities.

'I originally thought it could be a trick, but I dismissed that later,' Alexander says today. 'We even had magicians involved in looking at Geller. The idea of him relying on sleight of hand is nonsense. He is, of course, extremely gregarious and an extreme extrovert, and that worked against him, although had he not been an extrovert, the chances are that nobody would have heard of him.

'From the military perspective,' he continues, 'Macro PK [like spoon bending] was of interest to some of us. The smart-ass question from the sceptics would usually be, "What are you going to do, bend tank barrels?" I always felt that showed their limited ability to think about topics that exceeded their realm of knowledge. My response was, "No! I think what we're going to go after are computers." If we believed that PK was real, and some of us did, then the threat was to moving small numbers of electrons, not large objects. That was the most energy efficient concept.'

There was no need, Alexander explained, to take every computer down. 'All you have to do is make them unreliable, because everything we have is based on computer models

Colonel John Alexander, who taught spoon bending to US army officers.

and applications. So if you get to when you don't trust those computers and, basically, everything we run now on digital information, that would be really significant. We couldn't explain the process by which PK might influence computers. But we did theorize that unlike hit-to-kill mechanisms, PK had an additional advantage. That is, it didn't have to work every time. Making weapons and sensor systems unreliable

74

would be sufficient to have a devastating effect on the battlefield. Some took us seriously, others did not. At any rate, a few experiments were actually conducted after those of us involved either retired or moved to other assignments.'

Some of these experiments on using psychics to affect electronics were conducted as part of the Army's Stargate project, according to Paul Smith, a captain – and remote viewer – on the team at Fort Meade. 'There is some evidence that a certain kind of remote influence does work,' he told BBC TV director Vikram Jayanti in his documentary, *The Secret Life of Uri Geller*. 'That would, for example, be – well, the things that Uri Geller did – bending spoons, getting clocks to run, that kind of stuff. That's a form of remote influence. And the PEAR Lab, Princeton Engineering Anomalies Research Laboratory, that ran for 27 years at Princeton University, has very strong evidence of people being able to influence the internal operations of a computer.'

One method Alexander used in the 1970s and 80s to proselytize on for psychokinesis as a military tool was something called a 'PK party'. This concept had been invented by an introverted Boeing aeronautical and astronautical engineer called Jack Houck, who died in 2013. Houck developed a theory that metal bending was a metaphor for the power of the mind to do everything from maximizing creativity, to self-curing disease, to extracting rusty bolts from machinery. And he was convinced that anyone's mind could be trained truly to interact with molecules of material.

Houck became interested in Puthoff and Targ's remote-viewing programme, read all their papers, and began to do his own research into the subject. One aspect of it in particular, which he found out about through military contacts, fascinated him especially. This was the highly secret 'precognitive' remote viewing – the strange glimpses of the future (and, sometimes, the past, too) – that remote viewers like Geller and others seemed to display.

Houck began doing his own work, in parallel with Targ and Puthoff, with their cooperation. In one experiment he ran, a remote viewer described a randomly selected set of coordinates in the Caribbean, but with the alarming detail of a harrowing shipwreck, in which he sensed dozens of people dying. Houck discovered that such a passenger boat accident had indeed happened at this spot, but nine years earlier.

He developed a theory that certain 'peak emotional events' (PEEs) could transcend the boundaries of the known dimensions, that, as he puts in it his own engineering terms, 'If you add an emotional vector to the space/time vectors, you have the start of the way things work.' As an extension of that idea, he wondered whether you could actually create a paranormal event by inducing a highly emotional state – a PEE – in someone.

Houck discussed this idea at the various university parapsychology departments where his gathering new interest was taking him, and over time devised the PK party. Working with a metallurgist he was friendly with at work, he invited 21 people for a Monday evening event at his house. About half were proven remote viewers, half simply friends from his tennis club, all asked to take part in an unspecified experiment.

The surprised guests were each given either a fork or a spoon and told they were going to learn to bend them like Uri Geller simply by relaxing and having fun. It seemed a ridiculous idea, but its very silliness seemed to do the trick and the guests, who mostly knew one another, were all soon chatting and laughing as Houck had hoped they would. The metallurgist then gave them some instructions: they were all to 'get a point of concentration in their head', make it very intense and focused, and then 'grab it and bring it down through your neck, down through your shoulder, through your arm, through your hand, and put it into the silverware at the point you intend to bend it.' Then they were to command it to bend, release the command … 'and let it happen.'

For a while, there was nothing. Then a 14-year-old boy, in full view of the circle of guests, had the head of his fork flop down by itself. Having seen this, almost everyone experienced, as Houck puts it, 'an immediate belief-system change', and

Some of the cutlery bent at Jack Houck's PK parties.

within minutes, cutlery was softening and flopping over in 19 out of the 21 guests' hands. The plasticity of the forks and spoons seemed to exceed anything in Geller's experience. People were tying knots in the tines of the forks, and rolling up spoon bowls as if they were leaves.

By the time he died, at the 360 parties for 17,000 people that Houck hosted, spontaneous bending was a common phenomenon. Seven- and eight-year-old children were among those bending tableware. So much cutlery was bent at Houck's parties that guests often didn't take it all home. Houck had suitcases full of grotesquely distorted spoons and forks that he could not bring himself to throw out.

As an engineer, Houck naturally tried to work out what was happening. He developed a theory that the energy that the mind somehow manages to 'dump' into dislocations and flaws that occur naturally in metal when it is forged softens it as surely as if I were heated to 425° Celsius. He even documented cases where metal was missing from spoons after they had bent. He said that although his thinking on the phenomenon was influenced by quantum theory to some extent, he was more inclined to look for straightforward engineering solutions. 'The only thing I don't know is how the mind dumps this energy into the dislocations. After that, it's just engineering.'

Reflecting the military's gathering interest in teaching regular, 'non-psychic' people to manifest PK ability as well as telepathy, John Alexander took the PK-party concept from California, where Houck lived and held most of his parties, to the centre of power, Washington DC.

'The reason for teaching spoon bending,' Alexander explains, 'was to show people that things could happen that they did not expect, and to emphasize the importance of that, particularly from an intelligence standpoint. It was important that they ensure that when they looked at unusual data of any kind, that they [the CIA] did not dismiss it just because they thought it couldn't be true. The overall problem with the professionally sceptical class of people is that they are very scared. If *psi* is true, their world view is incorrect.'

Today, 'disruptive technologies' are considered a good, progressive thing, but at a time when the pace of technological change was more sedate than now, this new science did not attract an enthusiastic following. 'I worked with an Army engineer once on a *psi*-related project,' says Alexander, 'and he actually came out and said, "Don't tell me something that says I have to relearn physics, because I do not want to hear it." But most of the sceptics are not that honest. They won't say, "I don't want to hear it." They will just say it's not true, therefore it isn't. When all else fails, ignore the facts. Data that doesn't fit is categorically rejected.

'We stressed to folks,' Alexander continues, 'that bending silverware is of very limited practical value. You can make mobiles and things like that, but as far as something to do, it doesn't make a lot of sense. What we did suggest was that it certainly impacts belief systems, and also that they could take and use similar kinds of energy for things like healing and other practical applications.'

How high up the Washington tree did word of the PK party spread? 'Well,' Alexander says, 'I had the Deputy Director of the CIA at my house in Springfield, Virginia, for a PK party. But compared to potential war with the Soviet Union, it was noise, so, no, we didn't have the President there.'

The most dramatic party Alexander ran was at a military camp for a senior group of US army commanders working in intelligence at various locations around the world, who had flown in for their regular quarterly meeting. 'We were using the Xerox training centre outside Washington DC,' he recounts. 'We had a session and there was a commotion over in one area. This guy, who was a science adviser at a civilian equivalent of a two-and-a-half-star general, turned his head, and his fork dropped a full 90 degrees.'

'I didn't see it, but the guy next to him did, and screamed, "Did you see that?" I said I suspected a trick, because there were a lot of people there who would have liked to see me fail, and I was waiting for them to say, "Ha ha! We did it. You don't know what you're looking at." So I was cautious. But by now, people were watching. And while we were all watching, the fork went back up, back down again, and finally went about half way and stopped. This is with all the generals and colonels watching, and the guy just put it down and said, "I wish that hadn't happened." It scared the crap out of him. Fortunately, we were sequestered, which means it was an isolated, live-in conference, and we had a shrink with us. But it took us a couple of days to put the guy together. His belief system was not prepared. He was based in Europe, so he went back to his station OK. What he did tell someone later was that he tried it once again at home by himself and it happened again, but by now, he was able to deal with it.'

These dramatic, challenging events – all of which, it must be remembered, were sparked off by Uri Geller being discovered in Israel and, later, arriving in the USA – were happening at the same frenetic time that the bizarre scenario at the Lawrence Livermore Laboratory in California, as outlined in Chapter 2, was unfolding. In the same period, Uri experienced something else which made him want to give up on laboratory work and concentrate, for the while at least, on his ever-burgeoning show business career.

He recounts being spirited off to a government installation where he was asked to do something quite bizarre. He refuses point-blank to say in which country this installation was – a refusal that perhaps indicates it might have been Israel, or possibly a US facility in Mexico – but is insistent that it was not a CIA operation. 'They took me to a laboratory. In this laboratory, which was a white room with no windows – maybe there was a chair and a table – and there stood a pig, a big pig. The scientist looks at me and says, "Okay, Uri, we're going to go out for lunch. Stay here with the pig and stop his heart."

Having been apparently suborned into this role as a kind of voodoo, psychic assassin was the last straw for Uri. 'I just could not believe what I was hearing. Of course it was a pig, because a pig has a very similar heart to a human being. I was just so stunned. I had become a vegetarian many years before, and I love animals. And I was shattered, actually, by this request. It was like everything toppled down on me. It felt like it was the destruction of everything I'd done so far.'

A feeling that the ultimate target of the programme was Yuri Andropov, the long-time head of the KGB and who later became the Russian leader for a brief period, gripped Uri and grew in intensity. 'They were asking me to see if the power of the human mind could stop the human heart. I went into the room and talked to one of the scientists and said I wasn't interested in this at all, because it isn't in my nature to do such a thing. I was very quiet and very shocked. I asked to leave and they drove us – because this was a base outside a certain city – back to the hotel, and then I just flew back to New York.'

Chapter Four

I SPY

So if assassinating pigs (or goats, as in the partly fictionalized George Clooney film) by the power of thought was off limits for him, what specifically, do we know Uri Geller did do as a spy in the years after his non-specified intelligence work back in Israel?

Eldon Byrd believed that in the run-up to his arrival in the USA at the end of 1972, Uri was asked by the Israelis to go to Munich, where the Olympic Games were to be held. 'I didn't know him then,' Byrd said, 'but he once mentioned to me that he was in Munich at the request of a particular person in the Mossad and had told them after sensing out the site before the Games not to send the Olympic team over and they did anyway.' On 5 September, ten days into the Games, a group of Palestinian terrorists, reportedly with the connivance of a few sympathetic German neo-Nazis, broke into the Olympic Village and went on to murder 11 Israeli athletes and a West German policeman. According to Byrd, Uri was 'really pissed off about that and he was saying he didn't want to work with them any more.'

In late 1975, two New York friends of Uri's, the concert pianist Byron Janis and his wife Maria, recall Ariel Sharon, then a retired major general working as a special aide to Prime Minister Yitzhak Rabin, meeting with Uri at their Park Avenue apartment and having lengthy discussions about Israeli matters. 'They were obviously prepping him for something,' Janis says.

Byrd recounted two other occasions he knew about of Geller apparently working with Israeli intelligence after his arrival in the States. 'One time, in 1976, Uri called me when he was in New York and said he had had an encounter that evening with someone who said they were from Israel who asked if he would like to do something beneficial for his country. They wanted him at a certain time the next day to concentrate on some latitudes and longitudes, and to think, "Break! Break! Break!" He asked what was there, and this person said that if whatever there was there was to break, or if Uri could interfere with it, it would be good for Israel. He asked me if I thought he should do it, and I said, "I don't know. Why not? It would be interesting to try and see what happens."'

What had already happened was that an Air France Airbus had been hijacked by terrorists and given shelter in Idi Amin's Uganda: 101 passengers and the captain were being held hostage. What was about to happen was that the Israelis went on to mount a daring rescue mission by commandos who flew in on four Hercules aircraft. Benjamin Netanyahu's older brother, Yonatan, was commander of the elite Israeli army unit on the operation, and was the only Israeli killed on it.

'Uri called me all excited later on,' said Byrd, 'and asked if I'd heard what happened. The successful Israeli rescue raid on

Entebbe had taken place, and he was sure the co-ordinates he had been given connected with it in some way.

'Uri kept saying, "The radar in Entebbe, there must have been radars there. Can you find out if there were radars at these points?" I said I'd try. I had contacts with people at the CIA. I called them and asked them could they find out if there were radars at these latitudes and longitudes, as they were roughly on the way from Israel to Uganda, and if they could find out if the radar was really knocked out or not. They called me back and said they didn't have any information about that. They said the raid as far as we know was conducted underneath the radars anyway and we have no indication that there were radars at those points and whether they were working. But Uri had called me beforehand to tell me about this, and then the raid happened, so I thought that was pretty good.'

Byrd was not suggesting that this conclusively proved that Uri's psychic ability had knocked out all radar on the 3,520 kilometres between Israel to Uganda, and Geller is – eloquently, perhaps – silent on the matter. But Byrd argued that it did suggest at least that a Mossad agent was in contact with him – and believed he could mind-hack electronics.

A balanced reading of the Entebbe raid and Geller's part in it is that he was almost certainly drafted in as a slightly peripheral – but easily activated – backup to simply evading the radar stations en route, or avoiding them by some other more conventional method. The most threatening of these radar stations were in Egypt and in Eritrea, where a state-of-the-art Soviet installation was in operation. Andrija Puharich said Uri was asked to block 11 radar stations in total. 'I can only describe his role as being a shield for Israel like the shield of David in the Bible,' the physicist said. 'Whenever there was a problem, he was consulted and would give his ideas and opinion. He would see things that might happen, could possibly happen and so on.'

The mad Idi Amin, Uganda's despotic ruler, admittedly not the most reliable source, did tell reporters that the Israelis had 'jammed our radar', and there was another curious hint about possibly unconventional methods being used on the mission, this one from an Israeli officer briefing the press in Jerusalem after the raiders returned safely from Entebbe.

'The main problem was to get to the terrorists with the biggest surprise possible,' the officer told the world's media. 'We used several tricks to do that, and once it worked, all the rest was quite simple.' Uri for his part does not discuss the raid, but has said, 'Use your imagination. Wouldn't I have been asked to do things of this nature? Of course I would.' (Interestingly, Israelis, even those who accept Geller's abilities are real, usually use the word 'tricks' to refer to them. The officer's press statement could perhaps be seen as a coded tease in this light.)

An unnamed expert on the Entebbe raid told *The Independent* newspaper in 2013 that the Mossad, with British help, had gained details of the specifications of the radar system at Entebbe and therefore knew the precise approach direction that would be blind to Ugandan radar. He hinted interestingly, however, that a Mossad disinformation tactic might have been to let it be thought Uri Geller had been somehow involved in blocking the radar to deflect any suggestion of the British involvement.

Byrd also told the author of another instance of Geller being used by the Mossad. 'Uri had been secreted out of the

USA by the Mossad dressed as an El Al airplane mechanic. In a 747, there is a way from the cargo hold up into the cabin. That way, they got him in and out without going through customs. He told me they took him back to Israel and flew him over some place in Syria two days in a row and said they wanted to know where a particular power plant was from his psychic impressions, and he told them. By gosh, just a day or so after he told me that, they bombed it.' Russell Targ has said that it is 'totally believable' that Uri had been used to help Israel's June 1981 air strike on the Osirak nuclear reactor site in Iraq, then under construction. (When asked about this alleged mission, Uri was taken aback. 'I really don't recall ever telling anything about this to Eldon,' he said. 'I wonder if he got it from some other source?')

It is late 1976 before corroborated evidence emerges of Uri being used operationally by the CIA rather than him being observed by it. For over a year between 1976 and early 1978 he found himself living in Mexico City as a sort of psychic aide to Carmen Romano de Lopez Portillo, known as Muncy, and the glamorous wife of the country's president, Jose Lopez Portillo.

Uri had been brought to Mexico originally for a TV show. After the show, Muncy, then the first lady-elect, summoned him to her home with a police escort, to meet him. Lopez Portillo's predecessor, Luis Echeverria, later welcomed Uri at a reception at Los Pinos, the Mexican White House, and Uri immediately felt an affinity with the country. Echeverria's oil minster, Jorge Diaz Serrano, had a hunch that Uri Geller could help the state oil company, Pemex, locate oil reserves it knew it had, and was anxious to exploit. Lopez Portillo put Serrano's hunch to the test after he became president in

January 1977. And it worked unbelievably well. Although Uri fretted that he had more or less guessed the site from a helicopter, he was spot on.

Geller's dowsing abilities, his financial mainstay from his mid-30s onwards, had been discovered in England by the chairman of the British mining company Rio Tinto Zinc, Sir Val Duncan, who had seen Uri on TV and invited him to his home in London. Duncan suggested that bending spoons might not always be the best way for him to make use of his talents. He later took Uri to his villa on Majorca aboard the RTZ company jet. There he passed onto Geller his surprising knowledge of dowsing – surprising for a man who had been an ADC to Montgomery during the war, and was now a director of the Bank of England.

Uri with Muncy, the wife of the Mexican President Jose Lopez Portillo.

Geller subsequently did well mineral hunting for RTZ in Africa, and was so successful with his dowsing work for Pemex, that he was granted Mexican citizenship. He and Shipi were also flown around with Muncy on private jets and given luxury penthouses complete with pools in the exclusive Zona Rosa to use, along with the plentiful supply of señoritas who were fascinated to meet the handsome young Israelis-about-town. Their main preoccupation was keeping it from Muncy that Uri was seeing many other – and younger – women at the same time as her.

Mexico City's Soviet embassy, not far from where Uri and Shipi were cavorting, was known to be the nerve centre of the KGB's spying operations in the USA, a major headache for the Americans. So somebody at the Mexico City CIA station seems to have had the idea of deploying Geller for intelligence work. His seemingly interesting connections with the Mexican establishment, which was a tad too friendly to the Soviets for Washington's liking, could be worth exploring, too. Uri had meanwhile befriended Roger Sawyer, a former US Army officer and now a consular officer at the US embassy in Mexico, who he and Shipi had met when they were renewing their US visas.

'He invited me to lunch one day and he said we were going to the President's house,' Sawyer says. 'I was a little bit sceptical, but I thought, "All right, we'll see where this leads." So we actually went to the President's house and we had lunch with the wife of the President of Mexico. And while we were there, the President made an appearance, said "Hello!' then excused himself because he didn't have time to stay for lunch.' Sawyer was fascinated at the level of Mexican society the young Israeli had penetrated, but as he puts it, 'It was a little bit above my

Uri and Shipi with Roger Sawyer, consular officer at the US Embassy in Mexico City.

pay grade, so I didn't try to get involved in those activities because I knew that that wouldn't end well for me.'

Soon afterwards, Uri says he got a call from an American identifying himself as Mike. Uri was surprised the man had the phone number of his penthouse but agreed to meet him at a Denny's chain restaurant in Mexico City. 'He said, "We know what you did at Stanford Research Institute. I've seen the reports. We know you can do certain things with the power of the mind. Can you help us?"' Uri confirmed that he could indeed do this. So Mike gave him two specific missions, offering, as he had been authorized to, the carrot of helping him and Shipi out with their still slightly tricky visa applications – not that Uri needed much of a carrot.

The first task was to report to Mike the names of the Soviet embassy officials Lopez Portillo and his ministers were seeing,

Washington continuing to be concerned about Mexico's friendliness with the Soviets. The second was more exciting to Uri. 'Mike explained to me that every ten or 15 days, there was a diplomatic pouch that goes out of the Russian embassy handcuffed to the wrist of one of the KGB agents and with secret floppy disks inside. Mike was also aware that I was able to erase floppy disks.' (He had previously done just that at Western Kentucky University under the gaze of the physicist Dr Thomas Coohill and word had clearly found its way to the CIA.) Mike then asked Uri Geller to hang around outside the embassy. He even gave him a pair of reflective, rear-viewing sunglasses to wear so he could keep an eye on the front entrance – while apparently looking in the opposite direction – and try to get a feeling for who was coming in and out that might be of interest to the CIA.

It was proposed that Uri, with his Mexican passport in the name of his mother's distant family, the Freuds, begin to accompany known KGB couriers carrying floppy disks back to Moscow on board Aeromexico flights. His job would be to sit close to the courier for the Mexico City to Paris leg, mentally erasing the disks for the duration of the transatlantic flights and hopping off in Paris, leaving the unsuspecting courier to board the Aeroflot flight to Moscow with the now-useless disks. The problem arose, however, that the KGB agents travelled in first class, and Uri, never shy to discuss finance, asked Mike who was going to pay for his – and the ever-present Shipi's – fares? Mike came up with the idea that he should drop a hint to the Mexican president that a couple of the rare and special Aeromexico gold cards, only given to Mexico's elite and allowing limitless free first-class travel to anywhere the airline flew, would be quite handy. In return, Uri would be more than happy to promote Aeromexico by wearing specially made Aeromexico-branded T-shirts around town.

Uri was never told if he had been successful on the first disk-erasing mission, but says it was telling that he was asked to do the same again twice more. If he had been successful, the consternation and recriminations within the KGB when their floppy disks from Mexico City kept turning up in Moscow blank or corrupted can only be imagined. Wiping floppy disks was not the only thing Uri did. 'I told them about drop-outs and drop-ins in at the Russian Embassy, and Mike also took me out to the desert to test if I could move a drone, a spy model aeroplane, with the power of my mind. I managed to do that too,' he says.

'I was living James Bond. I was living the movies. It was a fantastic feeling that, wow, I was doing something for the CIA,' says Uri today.

'It wasn't any more for the Mossad. It was for the Central Intelligence Agency, the one that I saw in movies when I was a child, the big symbol, the logo of the CIA.' He says alongside other tasks, like the drone experiment, he was also working for the Mexican government as a kind of psychic bodyguard, warning Muncy and her husband of possible plots or about people who wished them harm, and steering them away from anyone suspect. His success rate at this is unclear, but his stock in Mexico rode ever higher. He was made a Federal Agent for the Mexican Treasury by the president and given a beautifully engraved .45 calibre automatic pistol that he would carry with him on flights back to the USA, which as a federal agent of another country, he was permitted to do.

That permission, though, did not prevent him soon afterwards from being stopped by Customs at Kennedy airport and having his gun confiscated. Uri called the Mexican authorities, who in turn called the US Embassy in Mexico City, who got straight on to the State Department. A US Customs Special Agent, Charlie Koczka, was told to sort it out. 'That's right,' he says today. 'Uri Geller was working for the President of Mexico and he [Uri] came in with a very nice 45 automatic, although I am not a great devotee of guns and never had to use one against anyone. My boss told me he was getting heat through the State Department and I was given the job of getting Geller's gun back to him. Koczka met Uri on 57th Street in Manhattan, checked out his credentials and handed back his gun. 'I suppose in the spirit of gratitude, he invited me and my wife to his apartment and we started a friendship, and through the years we became firm friends,' Koczka says.

Even while in Mexico, Uri was able to continue making social inroads in the States, specifically into politics. At a dinner at Los Pinos for Henry Kissinger and Rosalynn Carter, the wife of the US President-elect, Geller wowed Mrs Carter by bending a silver spoon in her hand. He had been manoeuvred next to her by the CIA's Mike with instructions to impress the First Lady-to-be, the hope being that she would then mention him favourably to the president.

While at Mrs Carter's table, he offered to read Kissinger's mind and recalls Kissinger recoiling, looking worried, folding his arms and looking uncomfortable, pleading, 'No, no. I don't want you to read my mind. I know too many secrets.' Uri said he merely wanted to do his telepathy with his drawings party piece, which unfortunately, according to Uri, went so well that Kissinger asked sharply, 'What else did you get from my mind?' When Uri replied, 'I'd better not talk

Uri in Mexico City reading Henry Kissinger's mind after bending a spoon for a bemused Rosalynn Carter, the wife of then President-elect, Jimmy Carter.

about that here,' as a joke, Kissinger became quite agitated, causing an awkward silence that lasted for a few seconds, until Uri explained he'd been kidding. Kissinger nevertheless ended the encounter looking thoughtful, Uri says.

With Jimmy Carter destined for the White House, Mike decided, it seems, to try to get Uri right into the Oval Office, to establish a direct line of communication over his pet psychic-spies project with the president. Rosalynn was highly receptive; Kissinger had apparently been quite impressed. Mike promised to get Uri into the White House for Carter's inauguration in January. He wanted Uri while he was there to beam a psychic message into the president's brain to give funds to a paranormal programme.

It may all sound like an indeterminate mixture of a maverick, anonymous CIA field agent's fantasy mixed with Uri Geller's famous imaginative capacity, which had been both his making and breaking since he was a child. Yet when, on 20 January 1977, Jimmy Carter was inaugurated as the 39th President of the United States, Uri Geller was right there, at the White House. Rosalynn Carter apparently said, 'Jimmy, this is Uri Geller, you remember, the young Israeli I told you so much about.' Uri beamed his psychic message at the president, while shaking his hand, in his nervousness, harder than he had meant to. The president, Uri says, winced slightly and asked, 'Are you going to solve the energy crisis for us?' Uri says he cannot remember what he answered to this unexpected question.

Carter's openness to the United States investigating the potential uses of psychic research was borne out seven years later, by a report in the *New York Times*, which claimed that in 1977, that he had ordered a high-level review of psychic research in the USSR, and called Uri Geller in for a half-hour meeting in the White House to discuss what the Americans could do in response. Uri, again, prefers not to confirm the *Times* report. But it was Carter, who, in what must have been an unguarded moment, became the highest-level personality ever to confirm that the psychic programme had been intensified.

When a Soviet aircraft wend down in Zaire, Hal Puthoff, one of the lead SRI scientists who had worked with Uri back in 1972, said, 'We wanted to get it. And, of course, the Russians wanted to get it back. Since it went into the jungle canopy, they couldn't find it by satellite. So, in fact, Stan Turner, who was Director of CIA, who, of course, knew about our programme, said, "Okay! When in doubt, who are you going to call? Remote viewers. Find this thing for me."' Puthoff and Targ activated a psychic called Joseph McMoneagle, who closed his eyes, said, 'I see a river. I see a village. There are some mountains. The plane crashed just to the left of the river.' He then marked the crash site on a map. The CIA successfully sent a team to the spot and found the Russian aeroplane before the Soviets could get near it.

'We were told that that would never see the light of day,' Puthoff says, 'But as it turns out, after Carter got out of office, he happened to be giving a speech in Georgia and some aggressive student said, "Did anything happen that was really off-the-wall when you were president, or something that would really be interesting?" Carter said "Oh yes, there was a Soviet plane went down in Zaire and they got psychics to find it for us." So that's the only reason that ever came out.'

Meanwhile, Uri and Shipi's sojourn in Mexico, where they were enjoying the presidential lifestyle, came to an abrupt halt. Uri's social progress around the capital with Muncy set tongues wagging, not just among the Mexican elite, but as far away as in London's Fleet Street, where in February 1978, the *Daily Express* gossip column ran a tiny piece headlined, 'Bending the rules for Uri'. It suggested that observers in Mexico City were speculating that Uri's 'warm friendship' with the president's wife was thought to be on the point of precipitating a scandal, and talked of the pair 'behaving intimately' at a shared holiday in Cancun.

Uri swiftly received a call from the president's son advising him to leave Mexico for good on the next flight – advice that he and Shipi took. They were late for the first flight out of the country, but had an ace up their sleeve. After they'd waved their special, free first-class Aeromexico passes at the official manning the check-in desk, the aircraft, which was about to depart, was held at the gate for them. Being able to board an aircraft that was still on the ground, even if it was on the point of departure, was one of the privileges granted to the lucky few who carried the card.

Back in New York for a spell in 1977, Uri had his talents called upon by his new friend, Charlie Koczka, for an unofficial law-enforcement mission. From the summer of 1976 onwards, New York had been terrorized by a serial killer who had murdered six victims and wounded seven more with a .44 calibre revolver. Jack the Ripper- style, he would leave letters promising further killings, signing himself in one as 'The Son of Sam'.

'The authorities were getting nowhere,' Koczka says, 'and although this was not a US customs matter, I felt that I should approach Uri and ask if he could, through me, assist the New York City Police Department. I knew this police detective and Uri has the ability he has. So I talked to Uri, and he said in order to help he wanted something that belonged to the killer. He actually said if he could at least be exposed to one of the famous letters written by the criminal, it would help him.

'So the detective asked if this letter could be made available and the authorities said OK. Uri didn't want to read the contents. He just wanted to get what I would call vibrations from a personal item belonging to the killer. But while we were at the police station, some lieutenant said, "No! We are not going to let this happen." which was frustrating. The reason for this was that some other person who was 'psychic' had appeared in a photo, which later appeared in an exposé newspaper and the police department said they didn't want to be openly associated with psychics because they were scared they would get a bad name.

'So although they didn't know anything about Geller, they turned him down outright. So as plan B, Uri asked if we could go to some of the crime scenes where the killings occurred. We went in my private car to Forest Hills, and then another area on the way to JFK, between Brooklyn and Queens. Uri walked through these parks where the bodies had been found and got what I would say was a reaction, a vibration and he said, "Charlie, do you have a map of New York City?"'

Koczka had a Mobil gas station map in the car, which he gave to Geller on Thursday, 3 August. 'Uri called me on the Sunday morning,' Koczka continues, and said, "I think the person who is responsible for these killings lives not in the five boroughs, but adjoining them in Yonkers." So I called the detective and told him that for what it's worth, this is what he has told me.' On Wednesday, 10 August, David Berkowitz, now serving life for the Son of Sam murders, was arrested outside his apartment on Pine Street in Yonkers, NY.

Reflecting on the incident decades later, Charlie Koczka, acknowledged that it's hardly conclusive proof of anything, yet impressive at the same time. 'In law enforcement,' he explained, 'your exposure is mostly to people who basically don't obey the law. So you have a tendency to be hypercritical, almost cynical, and you fight this because you don't want to think ill of your fellow man because most people are honest. But law enforcement people just don't run into them. So when you hear of a psychic or something like that, it's almost normal not to believe the individual. You know … it's like … the hand is quicker than the eye. But I can tell you I believe Uri Geller has these powers. I know he doesn't use them always, because he invited me once to a racetrack and he wouldn't give me the name of the horse that would win. He has said many times that he believes this is a gift and a gift you can lose if you don't use it properly, so I have never seen him abuse his power. No! Uri Geller, I believe, is the real McCoy.'

Espionage-wise, things were to quieten down a little in the following years, but didn't stop entirely. At one point, Uri was asked by two counter-espionage agents in the FBI to go to a party out on Long Island where some Soviet diplomats were expected to be. His mission in this case was to try to use telepathy to beam the thought of defection into the mind of one of them. He does not know if the mission worked.

So, when William Casey, newly installed as director of the CIA made his out-of-the-blue call to Uri in Connecticut in 1981, as detailed in Chapter 1, it was the first Geller had heard in many years from the US intelligence community, although he had done work for other Western intelligence services during this period. But Uri's career has been characterized by constant comebacks, and in 1987, he was in action once more. Indeed, 1987 was the zenith of his years of what might be called political influence. In February of that year, Uri was to be found in Geneva at a reception hosted by the US Mission to the arms negotiations with the Soviets. A fortnight later, he was briefing a gathering of senior senators and congressmen, along with 40 Capitol staffers, Defense Department and Pentagon aides in a special room in the Capitol Building, which had been sealed to guard against possible Soviet eavesdropping.

Uri had not been at the Geneva reception as the cabaret (although he did 'perform' for the assembled company). He had been invited by Senator Claiborne Pell, then the powerful chairman of the Senate Foreign Relations Committee, in the hope that he could use telepathy to influence the Soviet negotiating team, especially its head, Yuli Vorontsov, into making some serious concessions to the West, preferably, as a first step, reducing Russian missiles in Europe.

Pell had been introduced to Geller, who now lived in Britain, by Princess Michael of Kent, who is a good friend of Uri's, as is her husband. So impressed was Pell, that he arranged a three-way meeting in London's Cavendish Hotel with Geller, himself and Max Kampelman, the chief US negotiator. The day after the reception, according to a full-page report in *Newsweek*, the Russian leader, Mikhail Gorbachev, made an unexpected new offer – the removal within five years of all medium-range nuclear missiles based in Europe. Geller was quoted as saying he was convinced Vorontsov had called

Photograph taken secretly of Uri's meeting in London with Ambassador Max Kampelman, who led arms talks with the Soviet Union.

Gorbachev straight after the reception, having received his ESP message.

Even with the *Newsweek* article to back it up, it sounded like the kind of story that would fall apart under serious investigation. Indeed, they got a few things wrong, according to Uri. He says the key meeting with Kampelman took place not at the hotel, but at an office in London, and that Kampelman requested – as Pell had done previously – that Uri beam thoughts about signing the treaty into Vorontsov's mind. Uri says he was so convinced that people would disbelieve this whole story that he stationed a photographer across the road from the office to snap him arriving and shaking hands with Kampelman as he left.

To check out this story further, before Pell died in 2009, the author visited the retired six-term senator at his simple, elegant home, overlooking the ocean in Newport, Rhode Island. In the room was a black-and-white picture of Pell with his friend, JFK, another with Lyndon B. Johnson, and another with the Queen. In a corner was a chair from the investiture of the Prince of Wales in 1969. On the coffee table was a letter from Bill Clinton, wishing his senior Democrat colleague well, and adding Hillary's best wishes, too, to Nuala, Pell's wife. Had JFK ever been in this house? 'Oh, no … I mean not often. He might stop his boat out there and drop by, but not formally. No! Only at our home in Washington.' So was this Uri Geller story really true?

'Well, yes, actually,' the senator replied. 'I was interested in parapsychology, telepathy and life after death. I had no ability or experience in this area, but I believed in it, and I would love to have had the experience. So I thought it would be fun for Uri to bring his dog and pony show to some of the American and Russian delegates at a cocktail party. I was interested in seeing what impression Uri might be able to make on the Russians, and I think they were mystified. I'll never forget the Russian ambassador, Vorontsov, later the Russian ambassador to Washington. Uri bent his spoon. Then he put the spoon into the ambassador's hand, and it continued to move. Everybody saw that. It was a key moment for me.' Whether Uri really influenced Vorontsov, Pell reasonably says he can't know, and that it would be highly unlikely for Vorontsov to know, either.

Uri was in his element. 'Al Gore was there next to me, Anthony Lake the National Security Advisor, who later became the director of UNICEF was there. The Russians didn't know who I was. I did a little chitchat, and then I got very close to Yuli Vorontsov. I actually stood behind him, and I did exactly what Senator Claiborne Pell and Max Kampelman asked me to do, to bombard him with the idea of signing the treaty. All I did is I looked at the back of his head and I constantly repeated in my mind, "Sign! Sign! Sign! Sign!" And they signed. Of course, I can't take full credit that I did it. I don't know why. But it worked.'

Nuala Pell also recalled Vorontsov refusing to give Uri his watch. 'What I remember was Uri putting the grass seeds in the palm of his hand and they grew. He did it in front of us all. We just couldn't believe it. Everybody was floored. I truly believe in Uri, and I think everyone did. The Russians just looked stunned. They didn't know whether to believe or not to believe. I know Claiborne's colleagues in the Senate who were on that trip never got over that. They couldn't believe that Claiborne got him there, and then he performed, and they were so impressed. It was the talk of the summit for

Left to right: Head of the US Foreign Relations Committee Senator Claiborne Pell, First Deputy Foreign Minister of the former Soviet Union Yuli M. Vorontsov, Ambassador Max Kampelman and Uri at the Nuclear Arms Reduction Treaty, Geneva.

some time. But Claiborne was very determined; he believed in Uri and was determined that other people should have the chance to see him too.'

'I'd seen that kind of thing before,' the senator explained, 'and thought it might be a conjuror's trick. I talked with that guy Randi once, and he said it was a trick, and he could do it too. [Randi was the Canadian magician who spent much of his career trying to debunk Geller.] There's a great depth of feeling there against Uri, you know. It's almost vicious. But Uri was far more impressive as a person. I think Uri is a very likeable, decent sort. I never felt he was at all dubious. I respect him. I think he has good ideas, and is genuine. I also remember how unless he was in full vigour, he couldn't make things happen, which I found most interesting.' Senator Pell remained friendly with Uri into very old age, and visited him in England. Uri remembers that he declined to accept a watch he wanted to give the senator on the grounds that the gift would fall foul of US corruption rules.

It was Pell who also arranged the meeting at the Capitol, for which the official agenda, for the benefit of any Soviet spies or their American contacts, was to talk about the plight of Soviet Jews. The meeting was held in the Capitol's only SCIF – a Superior Compartmentalized Intelligence Facility – up in the rotunda of the building. Pell's senior aide, Scott Jones, a decorated Navy pilot, had arranged the bug-proof setting at Pell's suggestion. Colonel John Alexander, who had been invited by the Commanding General of Intelligence in the Security Command, was sitting in the front row listening and watching.

'He [Geller] talked about the stuff the Soviets were doing psychically,' Alexander recalls, 'but everyone wanted him to bend something. There wasn't a spoon around, so someone went outside and found one in the guard's coffee cup. I was watching very closely. I had been trained by magicians by now, and I had watched Randi do it frame by frame and I could catch him at it. Uri took the spoon, stroked it lightly, and the thing bent up quite noticeably. He put it down on the top of this chair and he continued talking, and I watched this spoon continue to bend until it fell off the chair. There was never a time when Uri could have applied force. And even if the touch were strong, it would have bent down not bent *upwards.*' Although Pell says he did not think the meeting was a huge success, at least one important politician there did. Dante Fascell, Member of the House of Representatives and Chairman of the House Committee on Foreign Affairs, rushed directly to the library to read up on Geller. Col Alexander managed successfully to leave the Capitol with the bent spoon in his pocket. He still has it.

'I saw Uri do that several more times after that,' John Alexander added. I introduced him to Steven Seagal, and we did it there in Seagal's house, the inner sanctum of his bedroom, with all these old ancient Tibetan tapestries on the wall. [Seagal is the macho actor who has been described by the Dalai Lama as 'a sacred vessel'.] I don't think Steven has any doubt. His belief system is that these things can happen, although it goes without saying that this is not totally unique to Uri Geller.'

So, under Jimmy Carter, and with perhaps a record number of influential government figures receptive to the paranormal

Uri amazes Senator Claiborne Pell (*right*).

in no small part thanks to Uri's pervasive influence, serious discussion of unorthodox science had its heyday.

The Maine-based paranormalist researcher and document-ferret Gary S. Bekkum, through his organization STARstream Research, has brought to light numerous now-declassified US government documents referring to PK and reflecting a continuing feeling among a variety of exotically named official bodies that enemy psychokinetic action could be a very real threat. One US Army Missile Command report unearthed by Bekkum opens with these words: 'The term "remote perturbation" (RP) is used herein to signify an intellectual-mental process by which a person perturbs remote sensitive apparatus or equipment. RP does not involve any electronic sensing devices at, or focused on, the RP agent.'

The Missile Command programme, Bekkum discovered, was, quoting SRI again, 'to determine the degree to which selected personnel are able to interact with and influence, by mental means only, sensitive electronic equipment and to ascertain how this phenomena might be exploited for Army-designed applications ... In Phase I, a computer-based binary random number generator (RNG) was constructed ... in Phase II, subjects were selected and trials begun [to determine if individuals could affect the random sequence produced using their minds alone]. When all were completed, the SRI investigators concluded that there was an anomalous, unexplained effect on the electronic system which could not be accounted for by engineering considerations only.'

Bekkum writes: 'After reviewing the SRI-produced data, the report concluded, "... when considered in the framework of the existing database, it is difficult to disregard claims for the existence of remote perturbation." As for the threat implied by the initially positive results, the report recommended, "If the random-event generators appear to be vulnerable to remote perturbation, an effort should be made to determine if sensitive equipment such as internal guidance systems can be affected. There is also interest in the use of some RP [remote-perturbation] sensitive device placed in covert secure areas to serve as an intrusion alarm against these areas being compromised by enemy remote viewers." Other files describe a "remote-perturbation switch" and "remote-perturbation techniques."'

Another report, this one dated 1980 and found by Bekkum in CIA files is called *Remote-Perturbation Techniques: Managerial Study* and discusses the PK mind-over-matter problem in greater detail. It opens: 'In view of the obvious military value of being able to disturb sensitive enemy equipment, it is to the advantage of the Army to assess the validity of RP [remote perturbation, or psychokinesis] claims.'

It later reveals, 'Two separate but technically identical RP experiments on random-number generators were undertaken at SRI International and at the US Army Missile Command (MICOM). The director of this program is under the oversight of a committee of three senior scientist-managers at MICOM.' This trial, the report says, cost $400,000.

Yet another review, written in 1989 by a redacted official of the Defense Intelligence Agency, classified SECRET and entitled *Government-sponsored Research in Psychoenergetics*, explains why American intelligence officials tasked their scientists on the problem of psychokinesis.

Happy – and productive – days for paranormal researchers, then, but not everyone in US government circles was content with such things being funded by tax dollars. Colonel John

Alexander had become aware of theological objections, too, from those with various religious perspectives.

'These people believed the events were real,' he says. 'However, they were, "The work of the Devil." Therefore, the military had no business participating in psychic research. This position was made crystal clear to me at a briefing I conducted in the fall of 1987. I was addressing a science panel headed by Walt LeBerg, a former Department of Defense Director for Research and Development. At the conclusion of my presentation on certain anomalous phenomenology, LeBerg exploded. He literally screamed at me, "You're not supposed to know that. That's what you learn when you die!" I made a quiet, but snide, remark indicating I'd made a mistake and thought this was a science panel. As quickly as possible, I picked up my briefing slides and got the hell out of there.'

The issue raised its head again, two years into the Clinton presidency, in 1995. Senator Pell's aide, Scott Jones, traced living in rural Texas by the BBC TV director Vikram Jayanti, says a very senior science official at DIA who was also an evangelical, born-again Christian, had let it be known that psychic phenomena were incompatible with his belief structure. Not long afterwards, Congress officially terminated the US Government's work on the paranormal.

'It became an emotional, theocratic issue with a very important religious segment of the country,' Jones told Jayanti. 'Programmes can't survive like that. It's okay for them to kill a lot of people, but they can't kill them by psychic phenomena – you're going to have to burn them or blow them up. It's a bizarre situation, I think. It had to go away and what I hope, without knowing, is that it went away but it still exists.' Indeed, Jones hints heavily that he knows the paranormal work continues, only now, as he puts it, it will be 'deep, deep black.' 'I can't imagine that the military, or the intelligence community, would ever fully shut down something that might enable them to gather intelligence better.'

Whether Uri went deep, deep black too is not easy to say. He was certainly involved during the early 1990s in delivering to some US intelligence operatives in Washington a European billionaire who, for whatever reason, wanted to discuss a specific matter with the US Government – and was aware that Uri Geller had the contacts to be a go-between. It is known that Uri flew in the billionaire's private jet from the UK to Washington, refuelling in Iceland. In the dangerous, post -9/11 world, however, he is much more guarded than he was about even hinting at involvement in espionage. To have helped fight the Soviet Union is no longer a problem – he has become a big TV star in post-Communist Russia.

But the kind of bad guys a psychic spy needs to investigate in these troubled times make the old KGB look like gentlemen. So there have been rumours – some not even tacitly acknowledged by Geller – that he helped locate Saddam Hussein's mobile Scud missile launchers in the Iraq War. He is also said to have helped the US military find hidden tunnels in North Korea. In this respect, Uri does have a photo of himself in South Korea with US Army personnel, which suggests there could be something in the claim.

Post-9/11, however, it seems Uri was contacted again by his old spook friends. He singles out a call he says he received. 'The only thing that I can tell you is that I was reactivated by a person called Ron. I can't tell you what nationality, and what country,' Uri says. He rather likes the idea of having been a 'sleeper' asset for so many years, and says that 'probably another 150 people' in a few countries will have got the same call. 'But I must tell you, you know, if some people out there, especially the sceptics, think that there is no paranormal or psychical research or there's no remote-viewer programmes going on, they're dead wrong.'

Both Hal Puthoff and Russell Targ concur with this. Targ says he has heard that remote viewers from the Fort Meade programme were called back into action to help in the search for Osama bin Laden. Puthoff agrees. 'There was a lot of re-contact of remote viewers. Some of them were talking about this at remote-viewing conferences. In fact I was a voice, actually, to try to talk people out of doing that. Because after all, if there are terrorist cells in the USA, you don't want them hunting down remote viewers as targets.'

As for who Uri's mysterious Ron was, there is an assumption among informed observers that this was a CIA official named Ronald Pandolfi, who was characterized by the notorious Wikileaks organization early in 2013 as, 'the CIA's "Real-life X-files" Fox Mulder. Pandolfi, according to the *New York Times* was a senior CIA scientific analyst in the mid-1990s. Elsewhere, he is said as late as 2008 to have been working with the DIA under the Office of the Director of National Intelligence. Kit Green, however, who has known and worked with Pandolfi for many years, says that Pandolfi was *not* the Ron who 'reactivated' Geller after 9/11.

Further corroboration of a reactivation of psychic remote viewers, meanwhile, comes from Nick Pope, a former long-standing Ministry of Defence official in London, best known for having run its UFO project. 'Post-9/11, we were in a different ball game,' Pope says. 'Clearly people did start looking at some more exotic possibilities, remote viewing being one.

'One way or the other, the establishment in the UK has looked at all sorts of exotic phenomena. UFOs, ghosts, psychic abilities, antigravity, perpetual motion, everything that you think is science fiction, somewhere in the UK, someone is doing it for the government, for the military, for the intelligence community, saying, "Is this real? If it is, can we get this to work?"

Just weeks after 9/11, according to Pope, the Ministry of Defence commissioned a study into remote viewing, outsourcing it to a civilian contractor to insulate it from the MoD. The work was a trial of people claiming psychic powers to see if they could be usefully deployed in efforts to track down bin Laden and other al Qa'ida targets. The report, Pope says, ran to over 150 pages and was classified 'Secret, UK Eyes Only'. 'That is one of the highest classifications in the UK government, information the compromise of which could cause serious damage to the national interest. So I was quickly aware when I saw this study that the Ministry of Defence had taken remote viewing very seriously. And had made some fairly diligent efforts to research it, investigate it, recruit remote viewers and see if we could get this to work.' The results, Pope concedes, were 'a mixed bag.'

The Independent newspaper in London quoted 'a source with knowledge of the trial' as saying, 'I am sure Uri Geller was approached for this trial.' 'The use of psychics in intelligence matters,' Nick Pope told the newspaper, 'is what we call a low-probability/high-impact scenario. Even if it is a very long shot, then the ramifications of success are such that it is worth trying. It doesn't cost much to put a psychic in a room with a piece of paper.'

Chapter Five

EARLY DAZE

The Uri Geller story is complex and, at times, baffling. The filmmaker Ken Russell, who once made a movie, *Mindbender*, starring Terence Stamp and based on Uri's life, summed up the enigma of his subject during shooting. 'Was Geller genuine?' he was asked? 'Only God knows', Russell replied. 'And he's not telling.'

The real start of the mystery can be explained only by Uri himself, because he alone was there when it happened – although nearly 60 years later, a possible witness did come forward to (kind of) corroborate Uri's first, most mysterious and personal moment of a life that was to be filled with strange events and curiosities.

There is no balanced, moderate way to put it. Really, there isn't. But Uri Geller is pretty much convinced that late in 1949 or possibly early in 1950, he had a contact experience with some extraordinary force field in the middle of the day in a crowded quarter of Tel Aviv. Whether this was something supernatural, or a scientific phenomenon like ball lightning, or even something extraterrestrial, he has no idea.

It is characteristically brave of Uri, however, that for over half a century he has never wavered in anything concerning this clearly profound memory of what we have to assume was *something*, even if it was not quite a close encounter with a UFO. It has undoubtedly been a gift to his enemies and detractors, and yet he refuses to compromise it. Interestingly, it accords in some ways with early childhood experiences reported by other remarkable individuals and always involving a bright light. Joan of Arc was one such person, and such seminal events are sometimes referred to as 'Joan of Arc moments'.

The events, which over 60 years later he continues to believe, were the start of everything, occurred in the shady garden of an old Arabic house opposite the Geller's flat in Tel Aviv. The family, who had emigrated to the new state of Israel from Hungary, occupied a modest apartment three flights of cool stone stairs up at 13 Betzalel Yaffe, on the corner of the busy Yehuda Halevi Boulevard. Uri's encounter was in a shady, walled garden that then occupied a spot now taken up by a modern, eight-storey branch of the Hapoalim Bank.

Then, as now, this was a noisy, vibrant downtown area, packed with characteristic Tel Aviv, four-or-five floor apartment blocks, shops, offices and schools. There were scooters and motorcycles darting among the cars, horns hooting, people shouting and arguing in the streets, dogs barking, children laughing, old ladies scuttling, and delicious lunchtime cooking smells coming from every apartment. Considering the busy, built-up nature of the district, nature managed to put on an impressive show. The kind of gardens

Margaret Geller's 2nd floor apartment (on the right) in Tel Aviv, where Uri and his mother lived until he was 11.

where Uri was to have his own Joan of Arc moment are quite commonplace in this city – secret little oases, almost impossibly tranquil in such a frenetic setting.

'The garden had a rough iron fence, all rusty, and inside, it was wild, with bushes and tress and flowers and grass,' he recalls. 'It looked like no one had taken care of it for ten years. I suddenly heard kittens crying. My first reaction was to find them. I was very small, so going into the tall grass was like a jungle.

'The next thing I remember,' he continues, 'I felt something above me and I looked up and saw a ball of light. It wasn't the sun; it was something more massive, something that you could touch. It was really weird, like a sphere, but nearer to me, above me. It was just hanging there, shining and strobing, then gently and silently drifted down towards the ground. Then after some moments – I don't remember how long – something struck me. It was like a beam or a ray of light; it really hit my forehead and knocked me back into the grass. It was exactly like that scene in the John Travolta film, *Phenomenon*.

'I don't know how long I lay there. I wasn't scared. I was just eager to run home and tell my mother. Maybe I'd stayed there for another minute, not thinking, not wondering, not understanding. At that age, about four or five, anything and everything is possible for a child. To me, it didn't look like some kind of phenomenon or a paranormal occurrence or a UFO. It just happened. But because it was a bit threatening, because it knocked me down, I tried to tell this to my mother, and obviously she thought I was making it up. And that was the end of that. It never happened again.'

It would have remained an intensely private memory – one for people either to believe or scoff at – had it not been for a possibly intruguing new piece of evidence about Uri's past that emerged in 2007. It was surprising both to those who study Uri's life and power and to the man himself. A retired Israeli reserve air force captain, Ya'akov Avrahami, after seeing a BBC *Reputations* documentary on Uri, came forward to say he believed that at around this time, he had witnessed what had happened to Uri in the garden.

'I was walking to the bus stop, down the road next to the Rothschild Cinema,' Mr Avrahami said 'when I suddenly saw a powerful light, a sphere-shaped light, a metre in diameter, bright and dazzling. At the same moment, I noticed that from a building on the left, a small child coming out dressed in a white shirt. The light halted again and, as if it had senses, for some reason, it suddenly turned around and approached the child. The light embraced him.'

Uri assumed it was a hoax, but he agreed to meet Avrahami when he was next in Israel. 'He was an older gentleman, married with children and he told the story again. And it was the way he described me as a little boy with the white shirt and black trousers, which is what my mother always dressed me in, that convinced me. He remembers that I ran home and this sphere of light chased me, and when I got to the apartment building entrance, and went in the door, the sphere of light exploded on the building and left a black residue. He was so shocked that he couldn't believe his eyes. And when I told the story on the TV, he realized after all these years that it was me.

'So after 55 or more years of me repeating this story, because I know it happened, but being told all these years that it was my imagination, or I was hallucinating, for the first time in my life, someone was validating what I've always known occurred. It was a very emotional thing for me, this man coming forward. Doubts have often slipped into my mind about the incident, whether maybe I dreamed it. But it was always very, very real to me and now with this man's testimony, I know he's not lying and now I know it definitely did happen.'

There was another, slightly more earthly – but still highly significant – childhood incident that happened to Uri a short time after this, and had the benefit until very recently of a living terrestrial witness – Uri's mother, Margaret. And, this part of the story being of a Jewish mother and her only son, the incident almost inevitably involves soup.

'We were sitting down to lunch in the kitchen eating mushroom soup, or possibly chicken, I don't quite remember,' Margaret Geller, Manci to her family and friends, told the author when she was 85. 'All of a sudden, I noticed that the spoon in his hand was bending. I didn't know what happened. I thought he might have bent it on purpose as a joke, to make me laugh. And then he said he didn't do anything and, that the spoon got bent by itself. I just wondered. But I always had the feeling that he was not like other children. He very much liked, how shall I put this, to be independent and to boss around the other children, his friends. He was always the same, just like now.'

Uri's account of the soupspoon affair is in tune with his mother's. He recalls initially dipping some white bread in the soup, and then placing the spoon in his left hand – he is left-handed – and taking a few sips before any paranormal activity. But then, as Uri was lifting a spoonful of soup to his mouth, the bowl of the spoon spontaneously bent downwards, depositing hot soup in his lap, and then fell off, leaving Uri holding the spoon handle. He remembers calling to his mother to say, 'Look what's happened'. She replied with one of those things flustered mothers say; 'Well, it must be a loose spoon or something. 'I knew that was silly,' Uri says now. 'You don't get "loose spoons".'

Uri Geller had been born in a small hospital in Tel Aviv at two in the morning on 20 December 1946. The birth was entirely normal other than in one significant and disturbing respect. Margaret Geller had already been pregnant eight times, and on each occasion had had an abortion because her soldier husband, Tibor, did not want children, despite his apparent disregard for contraception. Uri would not find out about the extraordinary number of abortions his mother had undergone – and that he might easily have been terminated foetus number nine – until he was nearly 40, and his mother quietly slipped it into the middle of an unrelated conversation.

As an adult who believed firmly in life after death and reincarnation, it was as great a shock to Uri as it might have been to discover he was adopted. He had always felt he had some kind of guardian angel, and when he learned that he might have had eight brothers and sisters, the news made him wonder whether there was possibly more than one invisible protector there for him. Uri discovered on quizzing his mother that it had been her decision to say that this time she was going to have the baby: it was her strength and determination to stand up to Tibor that had brought him into existence.

Uri was named after a boy who would have been his cousin, who had been killed in a trolley-bus accident in Budapest. He says today he is not angry with his parents about the abortions. He argues that these were turbulent war-torn days, and people did things they might not otherwise have considered. He also feels that if the terminations had not happened, and his mother already had children when she became pregnant with him, it is most likely that he would have been aborted himself.

Tibor and Margaret had married in the still-operational main synagogue in Budapest in 1938. Unlike Tibor's, Margaret's family was not religious. She had been born in Berlin, to Viennese parents. Her family name was Freud, and if the Hungarian Gellers boasted that gypsy blood ran through their veins, giving them a touch of exotica, the Austrian Freuds could point out that her Margaret was a distant relative of the great Sigmund Freud.

Uri had nearly been killed as a baby by shard of glass caused by a stray British bullet fired in the sporadic street fighting and sniping in Tel Aviv that was common in the lead-up to Israeli independence in 1948. Even today, the stairway of the apartment block has bullet scars in its light-blue painted walls. The British squaddie's bullet came through a living-room window, under which Uri was in his pram. 'I remember the two shots, and I remember the glass falling almost in slow motion. My mother had put a little teddy bear next to me in the pram, and somehow it rolled over my face and it saved me. Maybe I would have been cut up, perhaps even killed.'

Uri Geller was something of a street urchin, given a lot of latitude to do his own thing outside by his parents, whose relationship had become distant and tenuous. His devastatingly handsome and always impeccably uniformed father was seen publicly with a variety of girlfriends. Margaret worked tirelessly as a seamstress to earn the little family enough to live on. At the same time as being resilient and streetwise, Uri was, by his own admission, a little strange.

He was fixated by space, almost, he speculates today, 'as if something was implanted in my mind' during his Joan of Arc experience. He had started to draw detailed space pictures, with astronauts sitting in rockets surrounded by controls and screens. 'Across our street was a junkyard full of huge old water tanks, and there, too, I used to fantasize. I used to crawl into one which was covered in big rivets, and pretend I was in some kind of capsule, floating in space.'

This was, it might be said, at a time when space flight was considered as an impractical absurdity, and the idea of a space capsule existed only in science fiction. It's an idea anyone who thinks Uri may really have been contacted by aliens might care to run with.

Uri recalls other strange phenomena crowding into his little world. The spoon bending was occurring only occasionally, and apparently at random, but was frequent enough for his parents to become accustomed to it; their minds were so full of wartime worries about survival that they seem to have look upon its significance as some sort of scientific oddity.

The first post spoon-bending phenomenon to affect Uri would make him a playground sensation at the kindergarten he attended around the corner on Achad Ha'am Street. Being the centre of attention immediately appealed to the boy, and a new and curious ability to affect the working of watches and clocks in odd ways was now manifesting itself.

Uri's facility with timepieces, he maintains, had appeared as spontaneously as his spoon bending. Shortly after Uri began school, Tibor bought his son a watch, of which the little boy was, naturally, very proud. Uri Geller grew bored by school almost immediately, and the watch, with its slow-moving hands, in some way acted as an externalization of his boredom. One day, he recalls looking at the watch and seeing it was time for the class to be over. But a glance at the wall clock showed there was still half and hour to go. Disappointed and assuming his watch was running fast, he

Achad Ha'am primary school, Tel Aviv, 1954. Uri appears far right, second row from top, check shirt.

set it back 30 minutes and forgot about it – until the same thing started to happen day after day.

One day, he actually saw his watch shoot forward and shouted out in class, 'Look at this watch!' He immediately wished he hadn't, because everyone laughed at him. He does not remember whether the watch was actually still racing ahead when he held it up, but he does know that the incident served as an early lesson that people could be very hard and sceptical, would not simply accept his word, and would not necessarily even believe what they saw what was literally staring them in the face. He decided he just had a weird watch, and wouldn't wear it again. His mother said she would buy him a better one, and after a few months, she did.

But the new watch was soon behaving as curiously as the first. One day, when the bell rang for the end of recess, Uri looked at his watch, and saw that the hands had bent, first upwards, so they hit the glass, then sideways. The same thing, with the hands of the watch bending up under the glass, would happen again nearly 20 years later when Uri appeared on a BBC TV show hosted by David Dimbleby, and instantly made a name for himself in the UK. Back in those early school days, convinced, now, that this was the spoon thing in another guise, Uri's response was to keep it a secret. When he got home, his father was there on one of his infrequent visits and asked sharply, 'Did you open this watch?' Uri swore that he had not, and Margaret told Tibor about the peculiar things that had happened with the first one.

Uri recalls Tibor and Margaret giving each other a look, before his father suggested taking Uri to see a psychiatrist to get to the bottom of what he called vandalism first against cutlery, and now watches. Tibor was openly angry about Uri's odd behaviour, but Margaret said that whatever it was Uri was displaying seemed like a talent to her. The visit to a psychiatrist never happened – probably a good thing for some unfortunate psychiatrist, who might have ended up, when his watch started going crazy, thinking it was he who needed help.

The weird, haunting thing in the garden, the spoons, the intense fascination with space, the watches and even the embarrassment of being laughed at in class all combined to convince Uri even at this early stage in his life that he was special, possibly even on some kind of mission for a superior power. 'It was real; it was vivid in my mind. I know to this day it was no childhood fantasy,' he insists.

While he knew that demonstrating his abilities to people could lead to humiliation, something was itching in him – understandably – to show them what he could do. But he developed what has been a lifelong characteristic of revealing himself in different ways to different people. And it was not nearly as simple as targeting gullible of suggestible audiences. From childhood, it was almost the opposite, and even today, some of his closest friends, who are absolutely convinced of his abilities being natural and not faked, have hardly ever – never in some cases – seen him in action. Nor have they particularly wanted to.

Somehow, he has always seemed to get more pleasure and nourishment from showing people who are suspicious but intellectually willing to be impressed. When, however, he senses people who will refuse dogmatically to believe, whatever they have witnessed, and insist there it is all trickery, he either fails to perform – embarrassingly on occasion – or refuses to. This is seen by some as proof that he does, after all, rely on credulous audiences.

To others, a key question comes to mind; does he rely on some kind of 'energy' (that great, misused word) *from his watchers* to make his seemingly impossible effects occur? This may sound like the worst kind of hippy-talk, but remember what the aeronautical engineer, Jack Houck, concluded decades after the first spoon had bent itself in Uri's hand about emotional positivity – happiness, in fact – being a factor in anomalous metal bending.

Consider, too, the words of William A. Tiller, Professor Emeritus of Materials Science and Engineering at Stanford University and a Physics Fellow of the American Association for the Advancement of Science. After seeing an especially on-form Uri at a conference in Seattle, Tiller developed the idea that Uri is a 'coherer' who, 'absorbs energy unconsciously given by others, and transforms it into the form needed to produce such spectacular psychoenergetic displays'. Tiller became convinced that this explained why Uri was consistently less successful with negative audiences from whom Uri is 'unable to tap their collective energy fields.' Throughout history, Tiller adds, 'charismatic individuals have been coherers and had a great effect on crowds of people.'

Back in the Tel Aviv of the early 1950s, Uri seemed to have found a coherer in the form of a little pal called Mordechai. A few weeks after the showdown with his parents over the second broken watch, Uri was eating school lunch, when Mordechai looked down at his watch and exclaimed that it had just moved an hour ahead. Prepared to risk all since he now had an independent witness with his own watch, Uri uttered what for him was a fateful short statement: 'I did that'.

Mordechai, naturally, argued that he couldn't have done – the watch had never left his wrist. Uri asked if he could take it in his hand, and, he says, just looked at it and shouted, 'Move.' He made it jump two or three times, and by the end of the lunch break, had a crowd of excited boys proclaiming that Uri Geller had the most wonderful trick he could perform with a watch. The memory of Uri proclaiming in class that something had happened that only he had seen was forgotten. The boys could see this with their own eyes, and couldn't have been more impressed. Uri, of course, would like to have explained that, actually, as far as he was concerned, it wasn't a trick; it was something far simpler. But he knew that might be going too far.

Uri rocketed in his peers' estimation. Yechiel Teitelbaum, who was in Uri's class and now runs a Tel Aviv cosmetics marketing company employing 300 people, confirms this. 'He was always different from other kids, very strange,' says Teitelbaum. 'He did a lot of things not every child can do, things beyond understanding; he left the impression of someone amazing, very sharp, very strong, very, very popular. He was always the leader, even in kindergarten.'

'We were together from four or five years old,' Yechiel Teitelbaum continued. 'He was always doing incredible things in the playground with wristwatches. I also remember there were stories about him stopping the big classroom clock, but in my memory it was the big clock in the teachers' room that Uri stopped. I don't remember him bending metal, but what left the biggest impression on me was something different. It was Uri's *telepathia* – how he would tell me exact things I was thinking about.'

This human telepathy first manifested for Uri's mother, as it did for Yechiel at kindergarten, with the boy's uncanny knack of saying things just before she was about to. It became yet another of the oddities Margaret learned to shrug off. 'She was accustomed to the idea of me being unusual,' Uri says. Among the premonitions he would have that went down in family history as accurate was one that apparently came to him on a visit to the zoo during which Uri felt uneasy and asked to leave. A few minutes after he and Margaret had gone, mother and son maintain, a lion escaped and spent some minutes running about terrorizing the visitors. For the first time, having a telepathic young son began to have its practical uses.

Oddly, spoon bending, even though it was happening with increasing regularity and was seemingly coming under his control, was something Uri avoided doing with his friends. But with adults, he was unstoppable. Margaret's main pastime was drinking coffee and eating cake with her girlfriends. Uri would often accompany her, to the distress of many Tel Aviv café owners. He would be quietly eating a piece of cake when spoons on the café table would start curling up. The waiters would whisk them away, not wanting to give the impression the cafe used bent spoons – or indeed attracted naughty little boys as customers. Margaret would explain to her friends and the staff that such things sometimes happened when Uri was around.

One of Margaret's Hungarian friends was a younger woman, Shoshana Korn, who was at that time working in a hotel in Tel Aviv. Shoshana, or Juji as she was known, became Uri's godmother.

'We were in a café on the corner of Pinsker and Allenby one day when Uri started to play with the spoons,' Juji recalls. 'He was five or six, and bent four or five coffee spoons double. 'I said, "Manci, I hope you have plenty of money to pay the café owner." Fortunately, the owner was amused. I said, "Uri, you're going to ruin your mother." He said, in Hebrew, that it just came to his head how to do this, but his mother wouldn't let him do it in the house. All the other people were amazed. And as well as being able to do these incredible things, Uri was very smart, too. He'd stop clocks and watches, too, but then he'd always start them again.

'Another friend of ours, Anush, said to Manci, "You know one day you won't have to work all night, because he's going to make a lot of money." Uri used to spend a lot of time with Anush and her husband, Miklos. I remember her saying you had to hide everything made of metal from Uri, because he'd bend it. Miklos was a handbag maker, and he would sometimes get angry with Uri because he would bend his tools and the clasps he used. But then he'd say, "I don't know what to do with this Uri. He's a genius."'

The final disintegration of the Gellers' marriage ended Uri's days as a city street kid. He was moved temporarily, to avoid the chaos of the breakup, to a kibbutz called Hatzor, far to the south of Tel Aviv near Ashdod, that specialized in taking in children from broken homes. Here, they would be lovingly looked after within a settled, nuclear family, perhaps start to mend psychologically, and maybe even develop a taste for the simple, healthy country lifestyle.

A Hungarian-Jewish family, the Shomrons, took Uri in just before he was ten, in 1956, and the family's son, Eytan, became his close friend. Yet, oddly, he did almost nothing paranormal to try to impress Eytan.

There were odd incidents, nonetheless. Eytan — who saw Uri bend a spoon only when they were both 40 — recalls Uri accurately predicting a crash at the neighbouring air force base.

'My brother Ilan remembers Uri telling him that an airplane was going to crash tomorrow, and it did,' says Eytan. Uri, curiously, remembers saying in class one afternoon only that he thought 'something' terrible was going to happen, not that it was a crash at the air base, just beyond the wheat fields. 'I suddenly felt something very powerful in me, almost like a feeling of running out of the classroom. A very short time afterwards, we heard this huge bang. We all ran out of the studying bungalow and across the cornfields we saw smoke and we all started running towards this jet on the end of the runway embedded in the ground and the pilot inside with blood all over his face. It was quite something, the first time in my life that I encountered someone dead or dying. Actually, he survived and months later, he came over to see us and tell us about it.'

One former kibbutz child, however, has a very vivid memory of Uri giving him a brief glimpse of what he could do. Avi Seton, who became a management consultant in Portland, Oregon, was walking with Uri from the dining hall to the swimming pool one day when Uri suddenly said to him, 'Hey, look what I can do.

'Uri took off his watch and held it, and the hands just moved without him doing anything. I'm not sure if he was sophisticated enough at ten years old for some kind of sleight of hand to be involved, and I clearly saw them move. For some reason, I got the feeling then and now that it wasn't something he could really *do*, but rather something that was *happening* to him. But the funny thing was that all I said when I saw this was, "Hey, so what." I think it was always going to be like that for him when he showed these things to kids. "Hey, that's good, but you want to see how high I can jump."'

Eytan Shomron believes all the time they were together back in the mid-50s, Uri was thinking of giving his friend some indication that there was more to him than met the eye. 'I remember once walking on a dirt road in a field of wheat when Uri asked me, if I had the ability to know where the snakes are hidden in the grass, would it make me feel better. There were a lot of snakes, and they were extremely frightening, but I said, "No, I wouldn't want to know." It was such a strange question. Years later, I thought it was an attempt to hint at what he could do, to signal to me that he was sitting on a secret.'

When Uri's mother remarried and moved to Cyprus with her new husband, Ladislas, a former concert pianist, new vistas opened for the young Geller. He could see his mother was happy for the first time in a long while. He could leave the kibbutz, which he wasn't keen on. And as Ladislas was quite well off, an end to the family's poverty seemed within sight. But there were other, more subtle, benefits.

Cyprus was a British colony, so the boy would learn English to near perfection, which would be of huge benefit to his subsequent career. He would also become familiar with American culture. He had an American girlfriend for a while, hung out at the American club, got to love hot dogs, played in a baseball team and very much took on board the idea that the streets in America were paved with gold. At the suggestion of the Greek Cypriot customs man Uri was processed by when he arrived by ship at Larnaca to settle on the island, he even adopted the English (but also Greek) name George, which he used for all the years he was to live there, from the age of 11 to 17.

Uri was developing a yearning to show other adults, independent of his family and more sophisticated than his mother's coffee shop friends, the strange things he could do. Among the staff at Terra Santa College, his Catholic boarding school outside Nicosia, he would find such adults. Among the more significant of them were Brother Mark and Brother Bernard, both former Navy SEALs and a certain Major Elton, an ex-French Foreign legionnaire who taught maths at the college. These were the kind of people he wanted to show what he could do – if only to be reassured that he wasn't a freak. (Among other important influences in his life that he met in Cyprus was, of course, the Mossad agent Yoav Shacham, the story of which appears in Chapter 3.

Establishing through third parties, preferably unrelated, that Uri Geller had special abilities as a child is crucially

Uri on the steps of Pension Ritz, Nicosia, Cyprus, aged 17, just before his return to Israel.

important in unravelling his life story. His major critics would one day assert that Geller's powers mysteriously manifested only in his early 20s, after he happened upon a magicians' manual with a teenage friend [Shipi] and the two together sensed the makings of a wonderful scam. But it is in Uri's Cyprus period, from 1957 to 1963, that we begin to encounter strong indications that he was fully formed long before his critics believe. The list of children, teachers and others who attest to having seen and experienced his abilities so early in his life, before he had met Shipi and before he had supposedly learned mental magic from a book is so long, and their memories so precise, that the much-touted argument that Geller invented his 'powers' in league with Shipi a decade later starts to look distinctly threadbare – ridiculous, in fact.

Cyprus was also, inevitably, the scene for other major influences to come into his life. One of these was sex – his first, and also enjoyable and successful, experiences occurred here. Another was show business. He met theatricals at his stepfather's motel, a 14-bedroom establishment at 12 Pantheon Street in Nicosia, bearing an ambitious name for a little place: Pension Ritz. The Ritz was frequented by visiting performers working Nicosia's busy nightlife scene – and Uri developed an affinity with them and their lifestyle. He says he showed some his spoon bending and watch-disturbing abilities, and they were duly impressed.

Another, odder characteristic he evolved was a fascination for the ghoulish. Cyprus was war-torn and dangerous for his entire time there, as an ongoing war between terrorists, both Greek and Turkish, and the British Army was being fought. Uri frequently witnessed dead and mutilated bodies and the aftermath of bombings, all of which had its effect on the psychology of a young boy.

Just a year after Uri arrived on the island, Ladslas died, leaving Uri's mother alone for the second time. Even so, he still looks on his time on the island as one of the best of his life. For him, it was mostly a time of ranging about on his bike, taking the bus with his beloved fox terrier, Joker, to deserted beaches, swimming, snorkelling and getting to know about girls.

Uri was first sent to board at the American School in Larnaca, where he was not happy, but he quickly picked up English there. His second school, Terra Santa, was in a safe part of Cyprus, in the hills around Nicosia. It was strict, run by monks and had fairly primitive facilities – but provided an education well up to highly demanding, 1950s' British standards, something that came as a shock to many of the pupils, especially the Americans. Yet Uri was content there almost from the start.

Characteristically, he didn't show much of his paranormal ability to the other boys there. One contemporary, Ardash Melemendjian, now living in York, remembers only certain little things that happened around the new boy, George Geller. 'The college was built in an area they called the Acropolis, all stone quarries and caves. We used to go down to these caves. They were quite dangerous, and we were told at school that some boys had got lost and died down there once. One time when we were trying to get out of the deepest caves we got badly lost. We were faced with three ways to go in the pitch black. Someone started to say something and suddenly Uri said "Shhh!" and everyone hushed. He thought for a minute and then say, "This way!" and we went straight on or to the left, whichever the case was, and then we walked a long way before anything happened. But suddenly, we saw a little circle of light, and it got bigger and bigger, and that was the exit. I'm sure the rest of us would have chosen another way. I don't how he did it.

'There were other oddities which when you put them together, even back then, just made you wonder what *was* this guy,' Melemendjian continues. 'He never once got a puncture on his bike, and yet we used to ride through the same fields, the same thorn hedges. I'd get them all the time, and end up sat on the back of his bike, holding my bike while he was peddling. We'd go to the cinema to see X-rated films. I'd go to buy my ticket and get told, "No! You're too young! Out!" He'd go to buy his ticket – and would be perfectly all right for him even though we are the same age and looked it.

'Another thing that we used to take for granted, never give a second thought to – he never revised for anything. You'd find him sat down with a textbook that we were supposed to be studying and he'd have a comic inside it. But when it came to overall results at the end of the term, you could bet your boots that he'd be top.'

Uri also became a basketball star, not just because he was tall and athletic. He had an ability, clearly remembered by Melemendjian, other boys and staff, to move the hoops to help them meet the ball.

'It looked as if it was vibrating without anybody at all touching it. You could see it move, I believe, a couple of inches when George was shooting at it,' recalls Andreas Christodoulou, who is still in Nicosia and working as a heating contractor.

One Terra Santa teacher, Joy Philipou, now in retirement in the London suburbs, remembers of Uri: 'He stood out.

You can't have gifts like that and remain anonymous.' Of the basketball prowess, she says, ' He *guided* the ball. He could shoot from almost anywhere. It never, ever missed the basket. Now that is a feat for an 11-year-old. From one end of the court to another, over and over again. I thought it must be my imagination, but several people began to talk about it.

We all saw the ball sway when there was no one near it, or sometimes the post would sway a few inches to the left or the right, whichever way he wanted it for the ball to go in. In truth, it was really scary. There's been a great deal of talk and argument. People would say, "Ah, no, it's just a fluke, someone must have pushed it." But then you'd see it happen over and over again.'

Joy also remembers him pulling off pranks in the classroom. 'For example,' she says, 'he did this clock-moving thing, not just on me but on other teachers. But for me, it took a long, long time before I put two and two together and realized that it was him that was doing it. I wasn't into the supernatural or anything like that, and I couldn't make out what it was. But whenever it was my turn to ring the 12 o'clock bell, I would have Uri fidgeting in the class, wanting to get out for lunch.

'The clock was behind me, an electric wall clock, about a foot in diameter. The class was in front of me, Uri sitting among them and he would be looking at the clock. I would check with my watch to make sure it was 12 o'clock, and it said the same. But as soon as I got into the staff room, they would say, "Why have you rung 20 minutes early?" I would say, "I can't have, look, my watch says 12 o'clock. But all theirs would be a quarter of an hour earlier than mine. It wasn't until I began to hear stories from other teachers that I began to find that Uri had something to do with this. One teacher had made him stay half an hour after every one else. She said, "You won't go home until the clock says 4.30. So he started to get up and leave, and she said, 'What are you doing? I told you 4.30." And he said, "But it is 4.30," and she looked at the clock, and it was.'

The young Mrs Philipou's fascination with Uri was probably exceeded by that of the more senior Julie Agrotis, an Englishwoman in her 40s married to a Greek, and who taught English at Terra Santa. Mrs Agrotis's interest was sparked when a story was going round the staffroom that Uri's test papers in maths bore a striking resemblance – mistakes and all – to those of a German boy, Gunther Konig, whom Uri sat behind.

Uri says he simply saw Gunther's answers 'on this greyish TV screen in my mind' by looking at the back of the blond boy's head. Uri had first noticed this 'TV screen' back in Tel Aviv; it continues to be his description of how he senses the conventionally unseeable and unknowable. He says images tend to 'draw themselves' on the screen rather than appear in a flash. The teachers, naturally, assumed he was copying by normal means, and made him sit in a far corner for exams, under individual guard.

But the copying continued; whoever was top in a particular subject Uri was weak in would find his answers mirrored in Uri's. Mrs Agrotis was a popular teacher, renowned as a softie who never punished children. She, nevertheless, had to do her turn of guarding the habitual exam 'cheat'. It was while she was doing so that Uri forgot himself one day and asked her about some incident in the market in Nicosia that was troubling her from the day before. She was alarmed, as she happened to have been thinking about it at that moment.

On another occasion, he says, he saw the word 'doctor' on his screen and for a fleeting moment, saw her in a doctor's surgery. He asked cheekily if everything had been OK at the doctor's.

Mrs Agrotis and Uri started to have long talks together after class. It was some while before he felt confident enough to do it, but eventually, he showed her how he could bend a key and a spoon. Naturally, she was astonished. She did a series of telepathy experiments with him. He would confide all his secrets in her, going right back to his early astronaut fantasies. He told her about the episode in the Arabic garden, and insisted, with a conviction that she may well have found oddly eerie and disturbing, that he knew instinctively there was life on worlds far beyond our solar system.

Occasionally, when Uri was sent to the stationery supply room on some errand, he would hear the teachers discussing him in the staffroom. One, he recalls, would say he was supernatural. Another would insist that whatever happened was pure coincidence. Others would say it was all trickery. He got a huge kick out of listening to them arguing and asking, 'What is he?', since, he says, he hardly knew himself. 'I was just a normal boy with friends, except I had a bizarre weird energy coming from me which seemed really to be mainly for entertainment purposes.'

As with all Israelis, as Uri approached 18 there was no doubt what the next three years would bring for him – army service. He was more than happy about this. Although he had only been to Israel to see his father three times during the seven years in Cyprus, father and son were still close, and Uri's twin male role models were now his father and Yoav Shacham, both men of action. Uri's immediate ambition,

Uri with his mother and Joker at the Pension Ritz Nicosia, Cyprus.

therefore, was to be a combat soldier, and then serve Israel as a spy. Margaret hoped he would become either a piano tuner or an architect. But would the Israeli secret service be too covert, too low profile for a boy whose biggest thrills came from hearing himself talked about in the school staffroom? His excitement since childhood at performing in front of an audience, his naturally extrovert personality and his contact with show business types at Pension Ritz combined to give him a strong impetus, incongruous alongside the desire to be a secret agent, to be a performer when he grew up.

Having left Israel as a confused and unhappy little boy, he came home a confident young man. He was in the unusual position of having no particular old friends to look up, and had the rather tempting option – something a lot of people dream about at this time of their life – of reinventing himself as anything he wanted to be. He was a fully fledged Israeli, but still an outsider for a variety of reasons, the perplexing supernatural powers being just one of them. So the idea of being in the Israeli Secret Service seemed oddly more suitable than ever.

That's why, in the winter of 1965, Uri couldn't wait to get into uniform and put into action Yoav's master plan to turn him into Israel's version of 007. November, the month before Uri's birthday, came. He went by bus to the processing centre in Jaffa, was allocated service number 9711 71, and by the end of the day, was settling into a tent at a boot camp with seven strangers. He volunteered immediately for the paratroops and a couple of days later, was on the back of a truck heading north for a location near Netanya and the paratroops' training camp there.

Weeks of running around the base at the double with an 18-kilogram kitbag (walking anywhere for the first three months on duty was forbidden), of obstacle courses and of lengthy marches (which Uri particularly hated) led to the purpose of it all – the first parachute jump from an aircraft. Paratroopers had to make seven jumps before they could wear the coveted red beret. Recruit Geller's first jump, on a hot day at a nearby airfield, went perfectly. But things went downhill from then on. On his second, he panicked and fell clumsily, jarring himself. A subsequent jump, at 4am in the Negev desert almost killed him. He was already edgy; he'd had a dream the night before that he was going to die that morning. It looked as if it were about to come true when he bumped into the aircraft after he jumped and his main 'chute got into a tangle. Then his second one stayed firmly unopened. Only at the last instant, with Uri plummeting towards the ground,

Uri in his paratrooper fatigues on a training manoeuvre.

did it open, and he landed, praying that he would never go through such an experience again.

Immediately after he got his wings, along with the maroon crepe-soled boots and red beret that were part of the paras' uniform, something incredible happened that only Uri witnessed. A shame, because it is such a shockingly bizarre story that if just one independent voice could have corroborated it, many of the doubts that surround Uri might have been scotched there and then, or at least become more muted, even though the story contains elements which sceptical minds could seize on. Why? Because, to be honest, Uri cheated ….

Practically nothing supernatural had happened to him or around him since he had come back to Israel. That part of his life almost seemed to be behind him, left in adolescence, as if the things that had been happening to him since he was three were, maybe, the type of poltergeist phenomena that occasionally occur around disturbed, unhappy children and vanish in adulthood.

Uri puts the quiescence of his powers at this period down to pressure of time. 'You are constantly occupied and busy in the army. You wake up at 4.30 in the morning, you have to clean your gun, you have to shine your boots, you have to quickly have breakfast and get off to manoeuvres. It's a nonstop three years. There is time for nothing except, maybe, to write a letter. My big moment of freedom was when I was able to dive into the canteen and buy myself the equivalent of a Mars Bar and take off the thin silver foil wrapper and just indulge in the taste of that chocolate melting in my mouth. That was my pleasure. There was no time for thinking.'

Uri's first assignment as a para, he says, was a 110km march into the Negev as a heavy machine gunner, carrying with two other men a Browning machine gun some 36 kilograms in weight. The gun was broken into three parts – body, legs and ammunition – for transport. The heaviest was the body, and it was Geller's responsibility to carry it. Worse still, to gain his corporal's stripes, Uri was going to have to parachute out of a plane with the gun's body, something that army tradition maintained was the hardest task in existence. Once down in the Negev, the team would be taken by truck further out into the desert with kit bags, then make the jump with the Browning equipment and march back 10km to their base camp carrying it.

It is, perhaps, almost part of the typical young man's make-up to get round rules, and as he prepared for the exercise, Uri hatched a plan to avoid the worst part of it. It turned out that in getting off with the deception he practised to do so, he experienced what he regards as the second most profound paranormal occurrence of his life, to be topped only by a staggering (and in this case semi-witnessed) event many years later in New York.

The Browning gun's heavy body could actually be broken down itself. If the heavy tube *inside* the gun barrel and the mechanism which fed the ammunition through were removed, the shell of the gun could be placed in its canvas bag so as it looked from the outside like the full body, but weighed 4.5kg lighter. Since the exercise of dropping with the full body of the gun was purely a fitness test, and they were not going to need to use the Browning after they landed, and since he was still edgy about parachuting after his near-lethal tangle of a few days previously, why not, he figured, remove the innards of the gun and leave them safely in his kitbag back at base camp?

He could then carry the canvas bag at a stroll on the 10km hike after the jump. He ran through the physical reality of this tempting plan as carefully as any magician plotting a complex stage event. He would have to make certain that none of his comrades got to carry the bag, as they would almost certainly feel it was underweight, and he daren't risk anyone discovering his secret. But – significantly again, for critics of Geller – he calculated that he could get away with it.

The jump passed safely. The case, which was heavy enough even without most of its essential contents, was strapped to Uri for the jump, and let loose on a five-metre cable for the landing, to avoid him being injured by it on impact. He packed up his 'chute and slung the useless Browning innards over his shoulder for the march. Soon came the first prospective hitch. Seeing Uri striding robustly ahead, even though he was supposedly carrying the lion's share of the Browning, one of his pals said, 'Look at poor Geller. He's carrying that bloody thing on his own,' and insisted on helping him.

Wary of protesting too much, Uri let his friend carry the bag up a hill. But far from realizing that Geller had cheated and wasn't carrying a full load, the young man misperceived the situation, and marvelled that he had never been able to carry this part of the gun further than a few hundred metres without a rest, but now could. He must, he puffed as he handed the gun back to Uri at the top of the hill, be getting stronger. Uri now recalls that he was having to try hard to stop himself from bursting out laughing when something made him practically throw up in fear.

A Jeep scrunched up alongside the group of men as they rested on a cliff edge. In it was a general and some staff officers. Uri knew at once that the game was up. Very occasionally on such a dummy run, the commanders would spring a surprise on a random bunch of soldiers, and put them through a full-blooded manoeuvre, in which they would have to shoot with live ammunition at an imaginary enemy ambush. It was an excellent way of keeping the men on their mettle even during a relatively harmless training routine, as well as giving them a chance to try their skills against the kind of danger that very well might face them at any time. It was 1966 and Israel had not been at war since the Suez campaign, ten years before, but a well-armed and angry enemy was never more than a few kilometres away, even in the heart of the country, down in its southern desert.

The staff officers ordered Uri's platoon to spread out and set up the guns, ready to fire. He was so petrified that he began to shake. He did not want to take the empty gun case, minus its barrel and firing parts, out of the canvas, but he had to. As he did so, his mind racing to think of some way out of his appalling predicament, he could see daylight through the thing. His companion handed him the ammunition belt, which he fed it into the useless shell of the gun before cocking the non-existent mechanism.

In despair, he looked again through the lid of the gun at the first bullet waiting to be fired with nothing to fire it. He hoped, ridiculously he knew, that something might have changed, or that it was a bad dream he was about to wake from. The first group was ordered to fire its gun; the end of Uri Geller's military career was seconds away. He would be taken away, court martialed and jailed, then, at the end of what would have been his military service, he would be dishonourably discharged. His father would certainly never speak to him again. He would have no friends beyond the riffraff he would undoubtedly meet in the prison camp – if he were not actually kept in solitary. His mother would doubtless take pity on him, but would never be able to hide her tragic disappointment, let down by her husband first, then her son. If he were lucky, a job as a street cleaner or a lavatory attendant might see him into old age. If he could not even find anyone to trust him that far, he might end up joining the few tramps and bums who existed even in such a young, vital country. The general and the staff officers were hovering just behind him. As his mind was in freefall, the sergeant major continued barking orders: 'Company B … FIRE! … Company C … FIRE! … '

Then he had an idea of sorts; it was not likely to work, but it was certainly evidence, for all the good it would do Geller, of the quick thinking the young man was capable of when his back was against the wall in the middle of a deception. He decided to take his small side arm, a standard-issue, Israeli-made Uzi, and surreptitiously place it next to his dead Browning. When the order came to fire, he would pull both triggers. The report of the Uzi would be feeble and too sharp to be mistaken for that of the Browning, but in the noise and confusion and cordite of so many heavy machine guns firing almost simultaneously, he might just get away with it. A bit of chaos, an instinct told him, might work wonders at concealing what he was doing, perhaps even from the eagle-eyed top brass behind him. They, after all, weren't expecting the *wrong* sound to issue from soldier Geller's Browning. They were expecting the *right* sound. And it was just, faintly possible that the ploy might work.

He heard the command to fire and pulled both triggers. What unfolded in the next few seconds was a sequence that he claims he still relives all these years later. He insists vigorously that it was not a fantasy or a daydream. Yes, he knows he was always famed for his imagination as a child; he admits willingly that he had a wondrous ability as a young teenager to spin compelling stories out of nothing and to keep an audience rapt; he needs no reminding that what he maintains happened out in the Negev sounds suspiciously like one of his science fiction flights of fancy. *Both* guns fired.

The spent cartridges spat out of the Browning until there was no ammunition left. His first thought was that God had intervened, and as he has never had any other explanation for it, that tends to remain his belief. An officer behind Uri, obviously impressed by the young man's performance, even leant down to tap him on the helmet and said, 'Good shooting, soldier.' Trembling, Uri put his hand on the hot gun, which was now dripping black oil, and kissed it.

In the whirlpool of thoughts that followed, there was no one he could tell, not even in the rush of satisfaction and good humour which swept through the men as the officers drove off, leaving them with a short march back to the camp. He had told his closest army friend, a man called Avram Stedler, something about his powers, and his dream of being a spy, but knew that if he tried to tell even Avram such a story as this, he would probably abandon Uri as a friend, or just think he was a particularly implausible liar.

What happened, or what Uri perceived had happened, would already be enough to unhinge most people. When Uri got back to the camp, he was naturally anxious to examine whatever it was he imagined he had so deceitfully left in his kit bag. And now came, if such a thing can be imagined, a still greater shock. He peeped into his kitbag and saw the barrel and firing parts of the gun, exactly where he had left them. He went back to the canvas bag to look at the Browning again. The case was empty, just as it had been on the cliff edge when the general and the officers pounced on his unit. He returned to the kitbag and drew out the internal gun parts.

The apparatus had been clean when he left for the exercise a few hours earlier; it was now oily and blackened – just as it would have been had it been fired. The mechanism had clearly been fired; it even needed cleaning. Yet Uri was certain it had not left the kitbag.

The sequence of events as he saw it gave Uri, to put it mildly, a few things to think about as he cleaned the gun. His mind was full of Cyprus; of the light in the Arabic garden when he was three; of the bent spoons; the telepathy with Mrs Agrotis. What had happened presaged the kind of bizarre madness that would happen around him – much of it with witnesses – over the coming decades. But in his tent in the Negev, anxious as he was to unburden himself, there was absolutely nobody he could share it with. Could he talk about it with someone else? Perhaps Yoav, if he saw him again?

Yes, but that would mean admitting the dreadful deception to his macho man, military hero. 'I knew no one would believe me. What would I say to someone? That I left the barrel in my kitbag and then it reappeared shooting? I just decided not to think about it, because it might make me insane. I thought, maybe I am crazy and I never really hid the barrel; I only think I did. But I know I didn't. I *am* a logical and rational person; I know my deeds. I don't take drugs, I don't drink, nothing can alter my consciousness or subconscious or clarity and thinking. When something like that happens you are amazed and shocked, and because of the shock, you erase it and try not to think about it any more.'

Uri's military service continued untouched by paranormal phenomena. He got his corporal's stripe, and was recommended for officer training. Sometimes, he says, a knife or spoon would bend on the table in front of him without him having tried to do anything. But so long as they went unseen by his colleagues, these events served as a tiny reminder of what he had come to believe by now – that he was under the protection of some outside force, which was unfathomable, but thankfully not malevolent towards him.

He went off to officer school. Out on a field exercise in teeming rain one day, he was overjoyed to come across Yoav Shacham in the front of a Jeep. Shacham was back from the Mossad and doing a stint as a paratroop officer. Yoav got him to jump out of the rain and into the vehicle. The two embraced. Uri was overjoyed to see his mentor and role model and Yoav and was delighted to hear that Uri was taking the path he was. He asked if Uri was still doing telepathy, and reasserted his feeling that Uri's abilities could be put to good use in due course. Uri confirmed that he still dreamed of being a spy for the Mossad. Yoav encouraged him to put all his effort for the moment into officer school, then to go back to the paratroops and establish a fine record there as an officer. Then they parted.

With the Six Day War brewing, Uri was promoted to sergeant. After the war started, his unit was ordered at 3am on Tuesday 6 June, to head for a point called the French Hill, between Jerusalem and Ramallah, to try to prevent the tough Jordanians getting supplies through to their much-feared legionnaires in Jerusalem. Although he was not to know the entire picture, he formed part of the northern jaw of a pincer movement designed to encircle Jerusalem. Ramallah was a cool summer retreat favoured by rich Arabs, and where King Hussein had been building a summer palace until the war intervened.

Uri had a feeling, he says, that he would survive whatever was to come. Somewhere on the road, though, where they were refuelling their vehicles from a tanker, Uri saw Avram Stedler and became convinced that his friend was going to die. 'Avram,' he called out, 'can I shake your hand?' Stedler was puzzled and asked, why. 'Just shake hands with me,' Geller insisted. He felt sickened, he says, by the burden of somehow *knowing* so much he was not supposed to.

Not long afterwards, it was Uri who was nearly killed on the French Hill. His unit was ambushed by a Jordanian battle group in Patton tanks. Sheltering in a graveyard, as hastily called-in Israeli tanks engaged with Jordanians and Israeli aircraft bombed the enemy, a bullet ricocheted into his left elbow. The impact shattered his elbow bone. Uri tore off his shirt off to see if the profuse blood was coming from anywhere else, and, thinking, despite the pain, it was only a flesh wound, he tied it up.

Minutes later, he watched as one of his unit's cannon-equipped Panhard semi-light armoured cars came head to head with a Jordanian tank. The Panhard's gunner was Avram Stedler, but Uri's friend could only land his shell to within a few metres of the tank, where it exploded harmlessly. Uri then saw the tank fire at the Panhard from close range and watched helpless as Avram's vehicle tilted and shuddered.

What he describes as a strange rattle could be heard before there was a rumble from inside the car, followed by smoke and flames. Uri and another soldier ran to the wreck to see if anyone was alive. The bodywork was red hot. The driver and the captain were dead, but Avram was still alive. As they pulled him out, an Israeli tank shell fired from a distance away hit the Jordanian Patton and destroyed it. The shock wave knocked Uri off his feet.

'I saw Avram's left leg was blown off,' Uri recounts. 'He was very pale, but conscious. As I dragged him, all he cared about was his penis. He kept saying, "Is my thing all right? Is it still there?" I opened his trousers and looked. It was all blown away with the leg. I lied to him, and said everything was fine. We got him to a house. He asked if there were helicopters coming.' Geller grabbed a walkie-talkie that had two bullet holes through it and called into the dead radio to pretend to ask for a helicopter with a *chovesh*, a medic. 'I said a helicopter was on its way to pick him up and he'd be fine. Later on, of course, I found out that he'd died right there.'

There was no time to grieve for Avram. The gunfire that was still pinning the group down was coming from a Jordanian pillbox above them, and Uri decided to lead a party up to knock it out. As they sneaked up the hillside, a Jordanian soldier jumped from behind a rock and shot twice at Uri from, he estimates, three or four metres, but missed. Geller pulled his gun up to waist height and looked the soldier in the face. He noticed he had a moustache before he fired accurately, killing him instantly. Some moments later, in the confusion, with shells exploding and bullets flying all around, Geller was hit again, this time really seriously, either by lumps of metal flying off another stricken enemy tank, or perhaps by bullets: it was never established which. He felt a blast, sensed something hitting his right arm and the left side of his forehead, and, as he blacked out, assumed with resignation that he was dead. He remembers being surprised at how easy it was.

Chapter Six

FAME

After the traumas of seeing his friend Avram killed, shooting the Jordanian soldier – something that was to affect him deeply – and being wounded and hospitalized himself, Uri Geller's military service wound down quite gracefully. He left hospital with his left hand and arm in a cast, but with the right healed. At a later date, he needed an operation to remove some bone from his left elbow, and still cannot stretch or retract the arm fully, but he was in relatively good shape for a wounded serviceman.

As part of his recuperation, he spent the rest of the summer of 1967 as an organizer at a children's holiday camp, called Alumin. And it was here he met the man who was to become his devoted and loyal *de facto* kid brother, lifelong business manager, friend and confidante. Or to put it another way: if by any chance Uri Geller has been pulling the wool over the world's eyes these past 60 and more years, Shimshon Shtrang is the one person on the planet who, as they say, knows where the bodies are buried.

Shipi, as Shimshon has always been known, was 12 when he went to Alumin; Uri was 21. His job was to supervise in the dining room and to keep the children generally occupied. So he told gripping stories and organized exciting and ambitious outdoor games. But Uri, who was still in uniform, also had a mission at the camp —to try to instil a feeling of patriotism in the children and encourage them to join combat units when they were older.

Shipi Shtrang today is an easy-going, smiling, patient man, who speaks slowly, says little, and has an aura of wisdom about him. He well remembers telling his parents on the phone about the wounded soldier who was looking after his group. It was not so much that he told good stories or invented great activities, the young boy would say, but that the injured soldier could perform extraordinary mental feats with his group. 'In between the stories, he would ask someone to think of something or draw something,' Shipi explains. 'The whole subject of telepathy and mind reading was really new to us, and I suppose we looked on it as magic tricks, as part of entertainment. But it was amazing.'

More amazed still was Uri, who was staggered by the results he could achieve when he conducted telepathy tests with children, and most especially with Shipi. Shipi would get numbers which Uri had written down and sealed in envelopes; the boy would then go upstairs in a nearby building, draw his own pictures and apparently be able to transmit them to Uri outside on the lawn.

Uri started showing the children metal bending and again, when Shipi was close, the distortion in the metal would far exceed that which occurred with any of the other children. The two experimented with nails, watch hands and any metal they could get hold of. 'It seemed to me that Shipi was some sort of a generator to me, like a battery. The telepathy between us blew the other kids' minds because I didn't know him well. It wasn't as if we were friends or relatives.'

This symbiosis between Uri and Shipi would later become a matter of fascination to sceptical investigators, who wrote (incorrectly) that Uri could *only* function when Shipi was with him. The story, still quoted as gospel, was born that Uri's 'psychic' abilities only appeared at this camp, that Shipi introduced Uri to a book he had on magic, and that the two jointly cooked up the scam which was to become the Uri Geller stage act. Some researchers even claim to know which book it was – a magicians' textbook, still available, called *Thirteen Steps to Mentalism* by Tony Corinda, which was published in England in 1958.

Uri being Uri, meanwhile, he was actually rather more interested in Shipi's 19-year-old sister, a pretty, green-eyed, strawberry blonde hippy-type, with a touch of the Faye Dunaway about her. He first met Hanna Shtrang at a parents' day, when the whole Shtrang family came over from Tel Aviv to see Shipi. Uri and Shipi demonstrated some of the psychic stuff they had been doing together in the camp, and Hanna was hooked, even though with her, the experiments did not work particularly well. For the next 24 years, Hanna would be Uri's on-off girlfriend, then full-time lover and mother of his children; the couple married in Budapest in 1991.

What Uri learned from the experience at Alumin was the entertainment value of what he could do. He also realized that even if things had worked out in the army, he would have been too extrovert for the anonymity of the secret service. So he thought a lot about whether he could be a professional entertainer in his last few months back in the army, the rather pleasant period which he spent driving around villages, chasing up – with great success, he claims – deserters and people who had not registered for military service.

At weekends and on leave, he practised his psychic stuff for the Shtrang family and a widening circle of friends. Shipi, although still only a schoolboy worked on the same project – turning Uri's abilities into a viable stage act. He even did his first paid appearance, at Shipi's school, which worked well. Significantly, he found, perhaps counterintuitively, that although people were suspicious of him, they still paid to see his act, went away having enjoyed the novel idea of a conjuror who pretends to be a *real* magician, and were sometimes powerfully affected by what they saw. Controversy, Uri and

Shipi, Hanna and Uri, late 1960s, Tel Aviv, Israel.

Shipi rapidly learned quickly, was not a drawback; on the contrary, it was their act's biggest asset.

After his service ended in November 1968, Uri, who had inherited his father's dashing good looks, also did his spell as a model and made inroads, via the photographers, into Tel Aviv's swinging, beautiful people scene. (His ads were less beautiful, something that can be testified to by anyone who has dug out studio shots for Kings Men underarm sticks, in which Uri is seen beaming as he applies deodorant to a hairy armpit, while being watched adoringly by some long-forgotten 60s' beauty with long false eyelashes and her head level with Uri's crotch.)

More importantly, Uri's professional psychic career was taking shape. Shipi, still not 14, arranged for more shows in other schools, as well as demonstrations at private parties. Each one earned them no more than a few dollars, but for Uri, the increasing frequency of the appearances made him more and more confident that the powers he possessed could, within a reasonable margin of error, be summoned up on demand. And the strange, unprecedented kind of show the boys had put together was playing amazingly well with both up-market and down-market audiences. Was it a science project? Was it a magic show? Who cared? It was a unique event to have at your party.

Uri began seriously to think that capitalizing on his strange abilities could make him rich – rich enough, he dreamed, even to buy his mother a little coffee shop. He had already bought her a black-and-white Grundig TV set and himself a fancy hi-fi, and, always a big eater, indulged his appetite for food almost to the point of becoming as chubby as he had at times been as a child. He also bought a second-hand

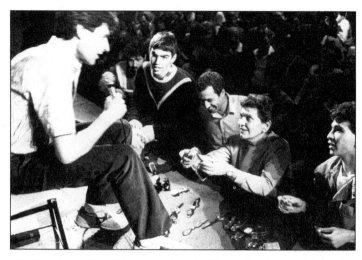

Uri's shows in Israel brought him an enthusiastic following. Seen here mending broken watches, brought to him by audience members.

Triumph sports car and told Margaret that if she wanted to work, she was welcome to, but from now on, there was absolutely no need. Uri was perilously close to being famous. He appeared in the newspapers. Theories abounded in the press as to what this man Geller's trick could be. Lasers, chemicals, accomplices in the audience and mirrors were all put forward as likely candidates. Fame, money, as much sex as he could handle with the pick of the Tel Aviv *belle monde*, and even a pretty, sensible girl waiting in the background to settle down with and have his babies. What more could a young man want?

His first fully professional stage show was in Eilat in December 1969, when he was approaching his 23rd birthday. Uri continued to insist that it was all 'real', but understandably, most people disbelieved him, assuming this was simply part

Uri next to poster for one of his very first shows: 'An Evening of Amazing Cultural Entertainment of Telepathy and Parapsychology', Eilat, 1969.

of his patter. Importantly though, even the sceptics were fascinated by his act despite their belief that it was based on trickery. He was managing, he estimates, a success rate with the bending, telepathy and watch stopping and starting of 70 to 80 per cent. Who had ever heard of a magician, part of whose success was based on his tricks only working some of the time? Even the cynics had to admit, it was a devastatingly clever idea.

But the most significant development, even if Uri didn't fully appreciate it at the time, was the interest in him from the country's professional and military elite. One unlikely new friend he made at exclusive social gatherings was the dean of the law school at Tel Aviv University, Dr Amnon Rubinstein, who was an academic with a flair for the media. He wrote for a number of newspapers and hosted a popular TV show called *Boomerang*, which covered the arts, science and intellectual matters. Rubinstein was not only convinced by what he saw with Uri, but went on to become one of his great champions, writing articles about him widely and inviting him on to his show.

Rubinstein became a prominent left-wing member of the Knesset, eventually serving as Minister of Education in Yitzhak Rabin's Labour government. He was introduced to Uri at a party by his friend Efraim Kishon, a respected newspaper columnist, who had been deeply impressed by what he had seen of Uri's abilities. 'Everyone was sceptical in the beginning, but these were amazing things we were seeing,' Rubinstein recalls. He speaks with great passion about Geller.

Like a lot of older, more experienced, better educated and, perhaps, wiser and more intuitive people who have been in contact with Uri over the years, Rubinstein felt deeply that the explanations, often backed by angry scientists, that the ever more voluble professional magicians were putting forward to counter any claims that Uri had 'special powers' were fanciful and smacked more of emotion than rationality.

'I had no specific interest in psychic things. I am a totally rational, sceptical person. So I am not a fall guy, but I am open-minded, and I saw things that I couldn't explain. I first saw him at Kishon's place and I immediately saw that there was something in it, that this was not mere conjuring,' says Rubinstein. 'He was not a trickster. I imagine the spoon bending is some sort of strange energy that we haven't even begun to measure, but I suspect it's subject to rational terms. I have since seen Uri do it hundreds of times. It has become almost routine. A magician told me that Uri supplies his own spoon, which is not true, but anyway, that wasn't what interested me so much.

'The thing that amazed me more than anything else is that he could write something ahead of time on a piece of paper and hide it, and would then tell me, my wife or my children or my friends to write whatever we wanted. It started with a very limited scope – any number, any name or any capital city – and without exception he was right. He could somehow plant a thought right in our minds. Then he moved on to drawings, and again, was right in detail, every time. To me this is much more significant than spoon bending. This was one single phenomenon, which cast doubt on many of the foundations of our rational world.

'There are things which cannot be repeated by any trick. It's one thing to be a David Copperfield, but here was something that was done in my own home, not in another environment, on a stage, which was organized and controlled as someone

Amnon Rubinstein in 1998, then a prominent member of the Israeli parliament.

like that would require. There was nothing there that could deceive me, and it happened so often. We invited him time and time again. He came into my office once, and one of the professors came in and said, "You're Uri Geller, but I know your tricks." So Uri said, "OK. Think of a number," and he said 'Ten thousand three hundred and something,' and Uri opened up his palm and it was written there. My colleague was staggered.'

The power and vehemence of the reactions of the coalition of magicians and scientists against Geller were remarkable, considering that a year into his professional career, he was not a household name, but was fast becoming one. Even so, the man who would soon become his first serious manager, for example, Tel Aviv impresario Miki Peled, had as late as 1970 never heard of Uri Geller. Yet the word was getting round among Israeli magicians that a fraud was at large, claiming that he had paranormal powers. Spoon bending was a completely novel trick, but for skilled sleight-of-hand conjurors, replicating it was really no great feat. Uri's supporters would say that replication by itself meant next to nothing – that just because there are wigs doesn't mean there's no hair. And it remains the case today, all these decades on – and something that still frustrates many magicians – that still nobody does it like Geller does.

Uri's appearance on Rubinstein's *Boomerang* programme, in accord with the show's name, came back on him. In the interests of balance, Rubinstein had invited a number of voluble sceptics into the audience. Uri, assuming a civilized discussion would ensue, started the show only to find the anti-Geller people howling him down. 'It was the first TV show I had ever done, and it would have been OK if they just didn't believe me,' Uri says. 'But they were attacking me, really violently, with personal abuse. It was the first time I'd had direct, physical contact with these people, and I was really scared. Then I realized it was in my power just to walk off, so I did. Amnon followed me out of the building and he actually started crying, because he believed in me so much and it totally devastated him.' The taped show was abandoned and never aired.

As he was cutting his unlikely swathe through Israel's intelligentsia however, Geller's relationship with Amnon Rubinstein almost hit the rocks in private. One of the agents Uri was working for at the time made the observation that if there wasn't soon more substance to his routine, people were going to get bored with it. He suggested that Uri 'fatten up the act', as he put it, by including a trick he had devised. Uri claims that he balked at the suggestion on the grounds that the very basis of his act was that it was genuine.

The agent, however, appealed to Uri's desire to make more money. His plan was to watch audience members as they got out of their cars outside the theatre, write down their licence plate numbers, and pass these to Uri, having shepherded the stooges to specially reserved seats. It was not a sophisticated scam. Uri began to use the licence-plate trick in his act, and it seemed to go down well.

The fraud was not discovered even by his detractors, but – and this surely says a lot about Uri – he confessed his guilt to Dr Rubinstein. It is likely that one of the many things troubling the young man was that by this stage he was starting to be taken seriously by elements in the Mossad and the Israeli military. To be unmasked as a fraud who had fooled them could be more than embarrassing; it could be dangerous. Uri says he went disconsolately to the law professor's office and told him to forget Uri Geller: that Uri Geller was no damned good. He explained what the agent had pressurized him into doing. Rubinstein then took Uri by the shoulders and said, part menace, part disappointment, 'Uri, you've done things neither you nor I can explain. You don't need to add tricks to it. All right, that's a trick. But how did you do all the other things? The spoons, the keys, the numbers and drawings you beamed into my head?' Uri replied with what many people regard as his strongest, least challengeable explanation: 'I don't know'.

Rubinstein confirms this account: 'I was very mad at him for this. I gave him a piece of my mind. I said he had deceived me. Even before that I began to suspect that he was using trickery, maybe mixing it in with the other things. There were a few things that I thought were foolproof, which couldn't be done by trickery, and now he was admitting to one. But then he was a young boy. To me the pre-cognition is much, much more important. I asked him how he did it. "Why is it so accurate? Why can you predict what I will be doing in two minutes?" He said, "Because I see. It is very disturbing." He said this is not a trick. He was adamant about that.' Rubinstein suggested to Uri that, in the light of this mistake he had made and the uproar his paranormal claims were clearly capable of making, he must sooner or later legitimize himself by having his powers tested by scientists. Uri took the message on board, although it would be a while before he did anything about it.'

His first brush with scientists was odd. In 1970, Miki Peled, his agent, was called by a man called Kelson, a physicist at Tel Aviv University. 'He told me he could prove to me that Uri was a liar,' says Peled. 'He invited me to come and see him in his house, and he was really angry with me. He said because of me, people might believe in Uri Geller, this liar, this trickster. He was a very strong personality and I was convinced that Kelson was right and Uri was a liar.'

Peled admits to being devastated. That evening, Uri was performing in Gdera. 'I phoned the theatre and said, "Uri after the show, please come to my house." When he came, he realized I was upset, and I told him the professor had said exactly what he does. I said, "I'm your friend, I'm your agent. I expect you to tell me, at least, the truth. I don't want to get the information from other people. I don't care if it's a supernatural power or a trick. For me it's good business. But I feel insulted that you don't behave to me as a friend, as a brother, as a father." And he said, "Miki, this Professor

161

Kelson is talking nonsense. I'll meet him and convince him he's mistaken." So now I was confused. "Ten minutes before, I felt you were a liar. Now I don't know. *Please* tell me how do you do it." He said, "I don't know how I do it. Sometimes I don't do it. I can never explain to anybody how I do it. My mother doesn't know how I do it."

'Two weeks later,' Peled says, 'we had a show in Jerusalem, and this Kelson came with all his colleagues from the university. They told Uri that they would be in the first row and would take pictures and tape the show, and make a big story in the newspapers about how he cheated. Uri said, "Please do." And some of them went on the balcony with a telescope. After the show I said to Kelson, "Do you still think the same as two weeks ago?" He said, "No, I think maybe it's a different trick. But our theories of physics don't accept his apparent abilities." We never heard another word from him.'

Itzhak Kelson, now Professor Itzhak Kelson, was anxious to distance himself from the business decades later. Like many of the scientists who pitted themselves against Geller, he was a lover of magic and had learned to do some tricks himself. But as keen as he was to spread the word against Geller in 1970, he was more reticent later. 'At one time, I believed it was important to persuade people that this was nonsense,' he said warily at his office at the university. 'Now, I try to disengage myself in a totally neutral manner... My energies are not channelled in that direction any more. It's obviously fraudulent, and that's it.' It was a strange reaction. One can only speculate on what caused his change of mind. Uri's stock with the country's elite, far above a young academic's standing, was rising vertically.

Indeed, among the ranks of Geller advocates and admirers were the country's defence minister, the war hero Moshe Dayan, with his distinctive eye patch; the just-resigned, but still-active and influential head of the Mossad, Meir Amit; the head of military intelligence, Brigadier General Aharon Yariv; General Ariel 'Arik' Sharon, later to be prime minister; the up-and-coming Benjamin Netanyahu, at the time of writing Israel's prime minister; the legendary foreign minister Abba Eban; the IDF chief of staff, Major General Rafael Eitan; and Brigadier General Ran Peker, a former Mirage jet fighter pilot and later commander of the country's air academy – not to forget the then-prime minister herself, Golda Meir. Even the newspapers were aware of Geller's dizzyingly lofty connections. They reported how Shimon Peres, then transport minister, later to be prime minister, had experienced his pen breaking in Geller's presence without Uri having touched it, and that Dayan had been meeting Geller secretly.

'Golda Meir and Moshe Dayan wanted me very much to work for the Israeli secret service, and to see how they could utilize my powers,' Uri says, and Meir even referred to Uri publicly, as we will see. Dayan also illegally used Uri to locate archaeological finds. Dyan, by now defence minister, had initiated the contact by inviting Geller for lunch at a steakhouse called the White Elephant at Zahala, where he lived. Geller did some telepathy with him, both the routine way, and the 'reverse' method that had so bowled over Amnon Rubinstein. Geller remembers both Dayan's single eye 'flickering and gleaming' – and that the defence minister let him pay the bill for lunch.

A couple of weeks later, Dayan asked Geller to come to his house for a more private meeting. This time, as a test,

Dayan said he had hidden a photograph somewhere in the room, and asked Uri firstly to indicate where it was, and secondly to describe the photo before he had looked at it. Geller recalls pointing to one book in a row on a shelf. Dayan confirmed that he had the right spot and asked Geller what the photo showed. He asked Dayan to 'project' the image to him, and Uri duly described an Israeli flag. Dayan laughed, which caused Uri to wonder if he had blundered. Dayan then turned to page 201 of the book, in which was placed a small snapshot of a flag flying over the control tower at Lod Airport. As Geller tells it, Dayan said, 'You've proved yourself, Uri. I don't want to see any more. There's no need for you to bend anything. Now what can you do for Israel?'

As for Golda Meir, Uri met her three times. 'Golda believed in these things,' Geller says, 'and she wanted to know the overall picture of Israel's future, and how many more wars were in store. She was very much for peace, and I told her I could see Israel signing peace treaties with all our Arab neighbours. I actually predicted it – but I don't know if it was a logical conclusion – that we were going to sign a peace treaty with Egypt first. I met Golda once in the Beit Sokhalov, which is the press centre, once at a party at the house of a friend, a general, and once on an army base, in a conference room in the barracks. I never visited her home. And the only time I bent a spoon for her was at the party.'

Just as Elvis Presley had to do his army service despite his world fame, Uri, as a minor celebrity and friend of the great and good of the little state of Israel, was required every year to serve in the army reserve. As he was still unable to extend his damaged arm, he would have been put on fairly dull duties, had not the Israel Defense Forces decided to exploit his unusual abilities and place him in a unit that entertained troops all over the country. This was a godsend for three reasons; it helped Uri become better known to people in captive audiences, who ordinarily might not have been interested in seeing him; it gave him a chance to bypass the conventionalities of rank and hobnob with still more high-flying officers and generals, thereby extending his networking still further; and it showed that he could perform without Shipi nearby.

Among the new friends he gained were two Israeli air force pilots, Gideon Peleg and Dov Yarom, both of whom went on to fly 747s for the Israeli national airline, El Al. They remain strong supporters of Geller. Peleg was a lieutenant colonel in the air force when he first met Uri in 1969. 'I met him at a party and later flew him to a show at an air force base at Sharm el Sheikh in the Sinai,' Peleg says. 'There were 200 or so of us there, a mix of soldiers and pilots. I remember they were very impressed by him. As a pilot, you have to watch maybe 200 instruments for the slightest deviation or change, so I think I see pretty well. And in all the hundreds of things I have very carefully watched Uri do, I have never seen anything underhand. Nothing.

'Privately, he did many things like driving a car blindfolded. He told me that he could see the road through my eyes and asked me to concentrate on the road. Things would move on the shelves in our apartment when he was there. When we were staying at a friend's apartment, there was a big old clock that hadn't worked for a few years and he made it move – he didn't touch it, but just put his hands close to it. One day, I remember, somebody showed him a picture of a group of people, and he pointed to some of them and said that this one has an injury on his left foot, that this one was very ill a few years ago, that this one broke his left hand. They were all correct. The guy that showed him the picture was amazed. Uri didn't know anybody there. Of course, I have seen the spoon bending on its own many times – these are the simple things that he does. But once, when we were talking about Uri in the kitchen when he was hundreds of kilometres away, a fork started bending, right there in front of us. I still have it. It was amazing. It was on the counter and suddenly we saw one of the tines just bend forward, several centimetres, completely on its own. But it wasn't scary, because we were used to these things after a while.'

Dov Yarom, then an air force major, had heard about Uri and came to see him at his mother's apartment to ask if he could do a Friday night party on his base. Uri was happy to. Yarom explained that the only issue might be a security problem. But Uri explained that he was already security cleared. This surprised the young pilot, but he was not in a position to know quite what inroads Uri had already made into the military establishment.

'I said, OK, so can you show me something? We were sitting head to head, and I didn't know about the guy. He told me a lot about himself, and was very confident, very persuasive, but I had to see. So he took a piece of paper and he tore it with his hands into a few pieces, put them on the table in front of us, and started concentrating. He put his hands 20-25cm above the pieces, and they started to float above the table, not very high, but moving. That was good enough for me. There was no fake involved. They really moved. I am very sceptical, I am very fond of magicians, but I always keep in mind that they create illusions. It didn't matter to me at the time if it was an illusion or a fake or the real thing. But as far as I was concerned, it was a real power. The same things have happened to me with a magician, but it's definitely not the same experience that I had personally with Uri.

'He took me over to the window of this four-storey building and he told me that he is fascinated by the powers he has,' Yarom continues. 'He told me wonderful things, astonishing things. He looked out of the window and said he can decide whether someone will fall in the street, although he didn't do it for me. Anyway, we invited him to the base and did all the usual stuff he does in front of the audience, but more amazing things happened later.

'We went to the house of one of our navigators. There were five or six couples there. So he started with bending a little spoon in his hand. It was very intimate, just us sitting having coffee and cake. He bent it in front of us. Really, it was unbelievable. He was holding it between his thumb and little finger and he had no power to bend it physically. And we actually saw the spoon bending. Another thing that amazed me was how astonished and happy he was when he succeeded. He didn't react as if he took it for granted that it would work.

'But more striking still was what happened to the wife of the navigator. She had very nice glasses on her head and he told her to take them off, to put them between her hands and cover them. Then he floated his hands over her hands, and said, "I have to concentrate. Help me with this," and then he said, "Open your hands," and she opened them and her glasses were bent. We were all astonished. She was not annoyed – there was no problem re-bending them. I know he wouldn't do anything harmful. Many years later, when I was flying for El Al and Uri was a passenger one time, he came onto the flight deck and showed everybody there the things he could do. I knew there was no way he would be a danger in the cockpit; I don't know, perhaps that shows that I was still a little sceptical after all.'

One intriguing assertion Yarom makes about Uri at this stage is that elements in the Israeli military became nervous of him as he darted from base to base, apparently overturning the laws of nature at every stop. 'He definitely had connections with some very high-ranking officers in the Israeli army. 'And as far as I know the air force regarded this phenomenon called Uri Geller as a security problem,' Yarom says.

'What they found a little frightening was that people believed in him so much. They were afraid of a Pied Piper effect, that people would follow him blindly. Because this guy was very persuasive, very trustworthy and very dominant and strong in character, if you are in charge of an air force that is dealing

Uri on a flying mission in an Israeli air force helicopter.

with a very technical, very real world, you don't want people to believe too much in a paranormal phenomenon. It's very nice if you go and see a magician, but it's totally another thing if someone convinces you he has real paranormal powers.

'In fact, it was the air force that first took the initiative towards trying to debunk him. They brought a few guys together who did something like Uri Geller did, bending spoons and driving blindfold – these three guys, I remember, were called the Ayalon Trio – and they were taken round the air force bases to say what Uri Geller does is a trick.' Eytan Ayalon, later chairman of the Israeli Magic Society, no less, launched a high-profile campaign of duplicating Geller's effects. He trained up two young men to act as fake psychics, grew a beard and told the press that Uri Geller would disappear if he did not announce himself as a fake within a fortnight. He went on to say that the group would 'reveal all'. Later, Ayalon spoke of his regret at this, but said it was a matter of 'saving the Israeli people'. A left-wing magazine renowned for exposés, *Haolam Hazeh*, also spoke of Geller, the 'telepathic impostor', as 'a national menace.'

Other magicians went on the warpath, but Uri still believes it is possible that this was part of a deliberate, military-inspired attempt to discredit him so he could work quietly on other things and the enemy be prevented from knowing for sure if Israel had a very unconventional secret weapon. The press was certainly loving the controversy; even the stuffy *Jerusalem Post* for 5 October 1970 headlined a story, 'TELEPATHIST GELLER TERMED A FRAUD'.

'*Uri Geller*', the piece read, '*a performer who has won a wide following as the possessor of "strong telepathic powers", was last night termed a fraud by four Jerusalem computer unit employees.*

'*The charge was made by one of the men, Mr. Yosef Allon, in an interview over the evening radio newsreel. Confronted with Mr Allon, Mr Geller told the radio interviewer he would have to "consult first" before deciding whether to sue for libel.*

'*Explaining how his suspicions were aroused, Mr. Allon said he went to a Geller performance and was as impressed as anyone else in the audience until Geller did a card trick that he, Allon, had been doing for years.*

'*A closer study of each of Geller's 'telepathic feats' was then made by Allon and three colleagues at the computer unit of the Government Office Mechanization Centre, Danny Zehavi, Yitzhak Ziskind and Alexander Eshed.*

'*Last week, they demonstrated the results by performing a series of Geller's acts before an impressed audience of the University psychology department. The four then explained that the feats of "thought transference" were accomplished mainly by sleight of hand.*

'*A member of the audience was Dr Moshe Capsi, of the University's School of Education, who had also seen Geller perform. He told the radio newsreel last night that the four were not only as good as Geller, but made fewer mistakes.*

'*Among the acts that Allon claims to have successfully imitated is that of driving a car blindfolded, allegedly guided only by the "concentration" of his passengers on the contours of the road. Allon declined to reveal publicly how this is accomplished.*'

What was going on in the background here remains open to interpretation in the light of what is now known about the extent of Uri's strong personal connections at this exact time – 1969 to 1970 – at the top of both the military and the Mossad.

On the one hand, we have Geller being close to the former, but still active, head of the Mossad, and the prime minister, the defence minister, a string of top military brass and fighter pilots all thoroughly convinced believers in his powers. We have him being given security clearance and operational missions by the secret service. We have a prominent professor of physics noisily pronouncing him a fraud, then immediately disengaging from the row he just started and even years later, refusing to discuss it. On the other hand, we have a core of stage magicians allegedly paid for by the air force to rush around the country telling servicemen to ignore what they've just seen – and also apparently briefing the press, along with other magicians, against Uri. It is not too fanciful to believe that the Mossad and others were, as Uri suspects, anxiously trying to put the cork back into the bottle and, for public consumption at least, discredit the man who was, if not their best weapon, certainly their most unusual.

Uri, however, was not one to be corked up. And in spite of the disinformation campaign hastily got up by ... well, whoever ... to un-convince Geller fans among the air force, he was forging on and making headlines. He managed a spectacular publicity feat at the end of September 1970, when Gamal Abdel Nasser, the Egyptian leader, died unexpectedly in Cairo of a heart attack. Nasser's death was one of the biggest news stories imaginable for Israel; his brand of Soviet-backed nationalistic socialism had been a thorn in Israel's side since 1954, when he became president.

The big news from Cairo occurred shortly after Miki Peled became Uri's manager, and upgraded the polish and theatricality of his act. The new partnership was going well, with theatres across the country that had previously seen 30 per cent occupancy reporting full houses for Geller. But however much more dramatic Uri had become in his presentation, nothing quite prepared Peled for the show of apparent hamming Geller displayed on the night of 28 September in a small Tel Aviv theatre, the Tzavta on Ibn Gvirol Street. From his seat in the stalls, Peled truly believed the boat which had so recently come in for him was on its way back out, under full steam.

Some way into the show, Geller suddenly stopped in mid-act, looked ill, sat down and asked if there was a doctor in the house. As one came up from the audience, Geller announced that he felt unwell and was unable to carry on because some enormous, historic event was about to happen. He elaborated, saying he believed Nasser had just died or was about to die. The show promptly stopped and Geller asked the 300 in the audience if they wouldn't mind leaving.

As they were filing out, looking puzzled and murmuring amongst themselves, Miki Peled was not a happy impresario. 'I just thought, that's it. That's his last show. Saying Nasser is about to die is not like saying it's going to rain tomorrow. There happened to be a journalist in the audience called Ruth Hefer, and I believe she went to the phone in the lobby and called the newsdesk at her newspaper, and then Israel Radio to ask what was going on. I think she came back and said there was nothing at all on the news wires about anything happening to Nasser.

'I was concentrating more on Uri. He was really not well. The doctor had taken his pulse and it was 160 or 170. If it was all an act, it was crazy. This wasn't something where he could say, "Oh sorry, I made a mistake." He was putting all his money on one number. If nothing had happened, people would have laughed for years. It would have been a grand finale.'

It is practically impossible to establish over 40 years after the event the exact timings involved, but the Israeli papers over the next few days were full of the story of Uri Geller predicting the death of Nasser 20 minutes, as they seem to have agreed, before it was announced in Cairo. There were, naturally, stories saying that someone backstage had happened to be listening to the radio and whispered to Geller while he was on stage that Nasser had died.

Uri maintains that it was just an inexplicable feeling he got, and a cool analysis of the whisperer-behind-the-curtain theory does not make it seem more plausible. Geller did not pretend to be a clairvoyant, so why would some backstage person, in the unlikely event that he was listening to the radio, tell a man in the middle of a spoon-bending, watch-starting, telepathic demonstration about the news from Egypt? Doing so might just as likely bring about a balling-out from the star after the show for putting him off his stride. And anyway, the news wasn't, by general agreement even in the more cautious media, on Radio Cairo until 20 minutes after Uri had made his announcement.

The Nasser incident finally turned Uri Geller into a nationwide celebrity. For anyone who had somehow not heard the show business buzz and also missed the Nasser story, Golda Meir finally ensured Uri's elevation to stardom. Asked by a radio journalist at a Jewish New Year press conference a few weeks later to speculate on how the next year would work out for Israel, Meir, probably delighted at the chance both to avoid giving an answer and to manage to sound clued-up, replied, 'They say there's a young man who can foresee exactly what will happen. I can't.' Geller responded later by saying that, in fact, he wasn't in the habit of predicting either.

'There was absolutely no question about it,' says Miki Peled. 'From the moment of the Nasser incident, he was the most famous guy in this country, and even now in a way, he still is. It was from this point that he became a phenomenon.'

Amnon Rubinstein, meanwhile, was still encouraging Uri to get into a laboratory before the wheels started to come off his career. He wanted him specifically to go an American or British university and have serious scientists examine him. For now, the closest Uri would go to a lab was to the workshop of an electronics expert in his neighbourhood called Meir Gitlis, whom he met at a party right back in his teenage years.

Meir, who had a reputation for repairing almost anything electrical, was fascinated by Uri's paranormal abilities and asked if they could do some informal experiments together. These had two lasting results. The first was that Uri was not a laboratory virgin when the first started being tested seriously by professional scientists. The second was that Uri Geller and Meir Gitlis continue to be partners in an electronics business, Nachshol, which Meir and his sons run from his combined home, laboratory and factory in a pretty village a few kilometres east of Tel Aviv.

Gitlis is a gadget fanatic with 30 in-production inventions to his name, among them, a metronome-like sensor to detect the tremors before an earthquake, a thermal diamond tester, an electronic dollar bill tester, a gold tester and a cellular phone radiation shield. 'At the beginning, I refused to believe in what Uri was doing,' Gitlis says. 'When he was young, Uri was always very naïve and excited when something he tried to do worked out, but I was still very suspicious. So I asked him if I could do some tests on him. The result of this was that I measured a voltage from Uri's body of about ten times more than average. What was more surprising was that he could make the needle of a compass move, even if it was your compass, and you put it where you wanted it. The compass could be on the table and Uri half a metre away from it and he could still make the needle move. It was unbelievable. I checked him carefully for metal and for magnetic fields, in case he had some magnet hidden, but there was nothing. And anyway, he was too far from the compass for a magnet to affect it. I often photographed the spoon bending. I was looking for the trick; but there wasn't one. I saw the spoon bend on its own many, many times.

'I told Uri always, "Look, I am a technical man. I believe only in what can be tested and seen." I often asked him when we were young, "OK, how do you do it?" It took me a long time until I believed that he was really doing it. I've seen magicians on TV saying they can do the same as Uri, but I can always see the trick. It's easy. But not when Uri does it. If you tested Uri and the magicians side by side, there would be no competition.

'My older son was very suspicious of Uri just like I was, and he did a telepathy test with him where he controlled all the conditions. He went into another room, and although the door was closed, surrounded himself with books so Uri wouldn't even be able to see if he was in the same room. Then he drew a car with a certain number of windows and lights and antennas. Then he went back to where Uri was and gave him paper and a pen. And Uri drew the identical car, with all the same antennas, the exact same length, only higher. Uri was on his own, without Shipi. These people who say he can't do it without Shipi are liars. They're just jealous.

'A lot of other things have happened to me with Uri,' Gitlis continues. 'We went to see our accountant once to talk

Uri's friend Meir Gitlis, the first person to test his abilities scientifically.

about something Uri wanted to do, which was to give all the royalties from our cellular phone shield to a children's charity. We were sitting in the accountant's office and Uri was under a light fitting high up on the ceiling, which was held up by a chain. And as he was sitting there, one of the links of the chain snapped. The accountant said the light had been there for 20 years without a problem. Uri also always phones when we're talking about him. We're used to that now.

'I once asked a neurologist I know what he thought the mechanism might be, how Uri works,' Gitlis adds. 'He told me that he believed the two halves of our brain transmit to one another on a certain frequency of some kind, and than Uri may have the ability to tune in to frequencies that are not his own, that his brain is like a scanner for these brain transmissions. He believes a very small number of people have this ability.'

It was, then, with Meir's small-scale, informal scientific experiments in mind as an example of how lab testing might be, that Uri spent much of his time in 1970 considering whether and how he might give a part of himself to science. It was no small matter that his show business career in Israel was beginning to fade to black at this time.

'I started ebbing away in Israel,' he acknowledges. 'My performances had a limit. I could do telepathy. I could bend a spoon. I could warp rings. I could hypnotize a little. And that's where it ended. A magician could write new acts, get new magic, do new tricks. I couldn't because I wasn't a magician. I was amazed when I started seeing the auditoriums emptying on me. 1971 was as incredible for me as 1970 had been, but already I was being attacked and questioned. 1972 was when I was over and out. People had seen me over and over, they were shouting, "Hey, Uri, we've seen that." Managers could no longer put me up in big theatres, so I started being booked into discotheques and nightclubs, underground, smoky places, with dancing and striptease and clowns, jugglers and acrobats. I was suddenly just another act. No one would pay attention to me, and I really felt the pits.'

Chapter Seven

I WANNA BE IN AMERICA

n Chapter 1, we met the unconventional Serbian-American medical doctor and physicist, Andrija Puharich, who came to Tel Aviv in 1971 to gain some initial scientific perspective on Uri Geller as a precursor to him possibly coming for formal laboratory testing in the US. Puharich was a friend of the Moon-walking Apollo astronaut, Edgar Mitchell, and it was officially on behalf of Mitchell's own research institute that Puharich was in Israel. In reality, Uri was being previewed, one might put it, by the CIA. Puharich claimed that he had worked for the Agency before, in 1948, on a US Navy initiative, 'Project Penguin' to test individuals said to possess psychic powers.

Andrija Puharich proved to be a both a blessing and a curse for Geller.

There is no doubt that it was because of Puharich that Uri came to America and embarked on the extraordinary period which led to him featuring in the leading scientific journals of the day, having private meetings with a president, spooking out a bunch of nuclear scientists so badly that they quit their jobs, becoming friends with a group as diverse as John Lennon, Salvador Dali and Muhummad Ali – and undertaking psychic missions for the CIA and the FBI.

However, it was also under the Svengali-like spell of Puharich that Uri became immersed in a world so weird that it would be an extravagantly gift-wrapped present to his sceptical detractors. But at least he escaped the fate of a previous 'project' of Puharich, an environmental activist and peacenik called Ira Einhorn who became a notorious murderer and fugitive from justice. Aged 73, Einhorn is still serving a life sentence without parole for murder.

So who or what was Puharich? He has been described as 'deeply eccentric' and 'bordering on the paranoid'. But if one word were needed to describe him, it would have to be 'polymath'. At school, he was an academic and sports star, excelling in the wrestling ring. He went on to do a first degree in philosophy at Northwestern University in Evanston, Illinois, working his way through college as a tree surgeon, before entering the University's medical school in 1943. His first medical assignment was as a second lieutenant in the US Army Medical Corps. He became deeply interested in parapsychology and ESP from the start of his medical career, but continued to lecture and publish papers on conventional medicine, too. He was also a formidable electronics genius, who hero-worshipped and modelled himself on another Serbian-American, the brilliant inventor, Nikola Tesla. And he was far from averse to a bit of fun; Puharich once played himself as a psychic investigator in an episode of the TV series *Perry Mason*, called 'The Case of the Meddling Medium'.

Just like Tesla, Puharich was megalomaniacal, neurotic, obsessive, manipulative and self-destructive. Just as Tesla did, Puharich patented dozens of inventions, many based on the newly discovered transistors and silicon chips. Among his patents were micro in-ear hearing aids that worked by electrically stimulating nerve endings in the bones of the skull, a device for splitting water molecules, and a shield for protecting people from the health effects of ELF (Extremely Low Frequency) magnetic radiation from the natural environment. Like Tesla, Puharich was adept at living royally on other people's money, although both men died in abject poverty. Both men also enjoyed the company of leading literary figures of their respective days: Tesla with Mark Twain and Rudyard Kipling; Puharich, 50 years later, with the novelist, Aldous Huxley.

In 1954, while the 60-year-old Huxley, who had been born in Godalming, Surrey, was living in California, he published his best-known work after *Brave New World – The Doors Of Perception*, an account of his tripping on the drug mescalin. The book became a bible of 60s' counterculture. Huxley borrowed the title from the poet, William Blake, and it, or part of it, in turn was borrowed in turn by a rock musician called Jim Morrison as the name for his new band – The Doors. And it was Andrija Puharich, the man who discovered Uri Geller for America, who introduced Aldous Huxley to drugs. Mescalin blew Huxley's mind, just as, nearly two decades later, Uri Geller, or so it seems, blew Puharich's mind – more or less permanently – and without using drugs at all. Paradoxically, since Puharich is so linked in the hippy consciousness with exotic substances, his new Israeli discovery, nice, neurotic Jewish boy that he was, was scared of both alcohol and narcotics and has always stringently avoided them.

At the time he sought out Uri in Israel, Puharich had adopted a rumpled Einstein look, frizzy-haired with a crooked bow tie. But in the 60s, when he first became well known in some sections of American society, he was an intense, handsome doctor, renowned as an author of books on the paranormal and as an occasional face on television. He served in the army again in the early 1950s, and in 1952, presented a paper entitled *An Evaluation of the Possible Uses of Extrasensory Perception in Psychological Warfare* at a secret Pentagon meeting. In 1953, he lectured senior US Air Force officers on telepathy, and the staff of the Army Chemical Center on 'The Biological Foundations of Extrasensory Perception.'

Puharich first heard of his protégé as a result of a lecture Uri gave to science students in the spring of 1970 at the Technion – the Israel Institute of Technology – in Haifa. When a retired Israeli army colonel named Yacov, who had heard about the lecture contacted a fellow Israeli researcher friend in Boston, Isaac Bentov, about Geller, Bentov wanted to know more. Uri liked the colonel and broke an ordinary little pin the man had while it was in his fist. The colonel mailed the broken pieces to Bentov in the States, who found something of interest in the structure of the break in the mild steel. Bentov talked about Uri at a November 1970 conference in New York for 'alternative'-type scientists, called 'Exploring The Energy Fields of Man'.

Delegates at the conference, Puharich among them, had been bemoaning the lack of a scientifically validated exponent of psychokinesis, Now in search of a new project, Puharich was soon on his way to Israel (and a discreetly hidden Mossad welcoming committee briefed to monitor what he was doing with 'their' Uri Geller) with a truckload of laboratory equipment and a mandate from the CIA to let them know what he found.

In 1971, while he had been raising funds for his Uri Geller fact finding trip, Puharich, had twice met Edgar Mitchell, the lunar module pilot for the Apollo 14 Moon mission. After serving as a back-up crew member for Apollo 16, Ed Mitchell retired and went full time into psychic and parapsychological research, writing a massive scientific book, *Psychic Exploration: A Challenge For Science,* and thereby earning himself the epithet 'half-assed-tronaut' from his non-admirers among the more crusading scientist and magician sceptics. The retired astronaut wrote to Uri recommending Puharich and enclosing a signed photograph of himself on the Moon. Uri had been obsessed with space travel even before there was such a thing and the very mention of Edgar Mitchell was enough to get him onboard for his first semi-formal, lab-rat duties.

It was, therefore, with some hope that Andrija Puharich found himself at 11pm on a hot Tuesday night in Zorba, a seedy Old Jaffa nightclub, watching Uri Geller perform as the climax to a succession of second-rate singers, jugglers and other cabaret turns – and being distinctly underwhelmed by what he saw. Geller knew from Mitchell's letter that Puharich was coming, but had not expected him to turn up at Zorba, and was embarrassed when he did. Puharich admitted to Uri months later that he was pretty sure at the end of his evening at Zorba that Uri was no more than a routine magician, and that he may well have wasted his trip from the States.

Puharich, although every inch the hippy icon, was not necessarily a credulous individual. The year before he discovered Uri, he had been to Canada to meet Arthur

Matthews, an 80-year-old man who had just published a book called *Nikola Tesla and the Venusian Space Ship*. It was Matthews' contention that Tesla, Puharich's exemplar, had not died as history recorded, in 1943, but was living aboard a UFO, which occasionally landed in Matthews' back yard. And it was Puharich's professional opinion after meeting him that Matthews was quite insane.

Initially dubious though he was of Uri Geller, too, Puharich installed himself in a friend's apartment, and over the next few days did some preliminary tests with Geller. Puharich, it seems, was determined to 'get a result' if there was one to get. He did so with the reputation and methods of the proper, pedantic scientific researcher that he was capable of being. He kept the most meticulous notes in a tiny handwriting on his Geller experiments, all of which were airmailed back to Edgar Mitchell. Precision note taking was second nature to Puharich; no tape recorder or film camera could be mentioned without its make and model number being logged; all times were accurately recorded to the second.

The events Puharich reported did, nonetheless, resemble a reprise of Aldous Huxley's drug-tripping research – and this was *before* Puharich's work in Israel with Geller turned seriously bizarre, as it soon did. It started routinely. Puharich explained to Uri that the tests would be lengthy and occasionally boring, but that this was necessary, thanks to the scientific convention that extraordinary claims require extraordinary proof. With Yacov, the retired colonel, and an Israeli woman friend as assistants, Puharich asked Uri what he would like to do first.

Uri suggested some simple telepathy. He wrote something on a pad, placed it face down on the table and asked Puharich to think of a number, then another, then another. Uri then asked him to pick the pad up. On it were already written the numbers, '4', '3' and '2', which Puharich had in his mind. Uri laughed, apparently delighted that it had worked. Like Amnon Rubinstein had been, Puharich was immediately more impressed with that than by the spoon bending, which he had seen at the nightclub and regarded as inconclusive. 'That's pretty clever,' Puharich reports he said. 'You told me this would be telepathy, and I, of course, thought you were going to be the receiver. But you pulled a switch on me.'

Uri explained why he had done it this way round, by saying that if he had told Puharich to try to receive the numbers, he might have fought him. 'In this way, you participated in the experiment without prejudice,' he said. Puharich asked if he could turn on the tape recorder and the camera. Geller assented, but added, 'You probably think that since I sent those numbers to you so easily, I might also hypnotize you to see and do things that are not really there.'

Puharich reported that he felt from that point the two of them would get along fine, although for several days more their relationship would remain formal, Uri calling him 'Dr Puharich'. After an hour of swapping numbers, colours and single words telepathically, Puharich and his assistants got into a huddle and agreed that, even if this obviously was not a proper, controlled experiment, they were satisfied that this was genuine telepathy. They asked if he could receive or transmit more complex data; he replied that he stuck to simple information, because then he could be judged wholly right or wholly wrong, with no grey area, as would be bound to occur if he tried to transfer whole concepts or stories.

Uri then asked if anyone had brought a broken watch. Yacov's friend said she had one which was not broken, but which she had allowed to run down and stop. Puharich intervened and asked to inspect it. With the camera running, he shook the watch, and it ticked for a few seconds, then stopped completely. Uri refused to touch it, and told Puharich to give it straight back to the woman. He placed it in her palm, which she closed. Uri then put his left palm over her hand, without, Puharich said, touching it. After 30 seconds, the watch was running, and continued to work for another 30 minutes before running down again. Meanwhile, Uri asked Puharich to take off his watch, a chronometer, and hold it in his hand. Puharich noted the time on it as 2.32pm, and then Uri held his hand over Puharich's for ten seconds and told Puharich to check it. The time on the watch was now 3.04; but what surprised Puharich more was that the stopwatch dial on the watch face had similarly advanced 32 minutes. For both dials to have advanced by the same time, the whole apparatus

Uri with Dr Andrija Puharich.

would simply have to have run for 32 minutes. 'This complex feat of psychokinesis was unparalleled in my experience, or in the literature, for that matter,' Puharich concluded.

The next day, Puharich repeated the telepathy tests with the same success, then asked Uri to concentrate on a pair of bi-metal strip thermometers. Even from across the room, Geller was capable of raising the reading on whichever of the instruments he selected by six to eight degrees.

Thoroughly convinced now that Uri Geller really did possess startling telepathic and psychokinetic powers, Puharich started to interview him about his past, and about his views on what his powers were. Puharich was impressed and surprised by the depth of introspection Geller, considering his basic education, had achieved. The core of Uri's own beliefs on the subject was that telepathic waves travel faster than light – something, remember, which only quantum physicists were aware was even possible, and even then, not unanimously aware.

If the light speed barrier were overcome, Uri suggested, then we could see into the past and the future, as well as teleport materials instantaneously. He also said he believed that the particles that existed beyond the speed of light were too small to have yet been discovered. On the question of teleportation, he did not discuss his extraordinary incident in the army with the heavy machine-gun parts that had apparently teleported to him in the Negev, but he did tell Puharich that when he broke a ring, it often lost weight, and how when he snapped a jewellery chain, a link was frequently found to have vanished.

Uri also speculated, Puharich reported, on what the source of his powers might be. One idea was that he had inherited them by some genetic fluke from a previous human civilization, to whom they were commonplace. A second theory of his was similar, but proposed that his ancestors had interbred with extraterrestrials. A third idea was that there was a simple warp in the make-up of his brain. The fourth, he said mysteriously, he didn't want to talk about, except insofar as it was related to idea number two, and that, 'They are somewhere out there. They have their reasons.'

Geller returned to the experiments. He promised to crack but not break a ring belonging to Yacov's wife, Sara, and did so, creating a fracture. Puharich sent the ring to a metallurgist at the Materials Science Department of Stanford University in California and several months later, he said, was informed that electron microscopy had shown the fracture in the ring to be of an unknown kind.

For a few more days, Puharich repeated the same tests again and again, determined, at least from his account, not to be fooled. He needed to go back to the States with sufficient evidence of Geller's abilities to guarantee that he, with Edgar Mitchell's help, could drum up more financial support for him to do further Geller research in Israel, with a view of opening up the possibility for Uri to be tested scientifically in America.

Puharich was back in Israel in November 1971 to try to find some answers to the fascinating scientific phenomenon he seemed to have uncovered in August. That mysterious reference Geller had made to Puharich back in August – *'They are somewhere out there. They have their reasons.'* – had brought to Puharich's mind something extraordinary that he had encountered back in 1952 when he was just an army medic with an interest in the relatively new field of parapsychology.

At a party in New York that year, Puharich met Dr DG Vinod, a professor of philosophy and psychology at the

University of Poona, in India. Dr Vinod was on a lecture tour organized by the Rotary Club. Vinod, like Puharich, was interested in ESP. Two months after meeting Dr Vinod, Puharich accidentally bumped into him again on a train. As they were travelling, the Hindu scholar did a past and future life reading for Puharich by holding his right ring finger at the middle joint with his right thumb and index finger. Puharich found Vinod's past reading uncannily accurate. On New Year's Eve 1952, Puharich invited him to his home in Maine, where, at 9pm, the Indian went almost immediately into a deep, hypnotic-like trance.

While he was in trance, Vinod apparently took on a deep, sonorous voice in perfect, unaccented English, which was quite different from his normal, high-pitched, soft, and Indian-accented speech. He said, according to Puharich's notes: *'We are Nine principles and forces, personalities if you will, working in complete mutual implication. We are forces, and the nature of our work is to accentuate the positive, the evolutional, and the teleological aspects of existence.'*

Vinod went on in this vein for 90 minutes, interspersing his monologue with references to Einstein, Jesus, Puharich himself, and a mathematical equation, which, amusingly, when examined by mathematicians was later found to be ever so slightly wrong. After listening to Dr Vinod while he was in trance over a period of a month, Puharich and a group of helpers were sure they were dealing with something more than messages from the spirit world. They were persuaded that they were being spoken to through Dr Vinod by an extraterrestrial intelligence, which Puharich named 'The Nine', supreme alien beings from far beyond our part of the Universe, who had turned their attentions to saving Earthlings from the disastrous consequences of their wars, pollution and so on. Puharich was convinced that the beings, rather than come in person, were using unmanned spacecraft to change conditions on our planet and to contact and train selected humans – starting, naturally, with himself.

At the end of January 1953, Vinod went home, and Puharich heard nothing more from him. Remarkable though the experience of being contacted by extraterrestrials must have been, Puharich seems to have managed to shelve it for 19 years – until, in November 1971, The Nine spoke to him again in Tel Aviv, through the medium of a hypnotized Uri Geller.

For his second trip, Puharich had rented a sixth-floor apartment in the up-market area of Herzliya, north of Tel Aviv, just over a kilometre or so back from the Mediterranean – Puharich was always rigorous about not stinting himself materially. He set up camp from crates loaded with the latest in magnetometers, cameras, tape recorders and countless electronic gadgets Geller could not identify, and started work again. It was agreed between the two men that Geller would give Puharich three to four hours a day, but that this might have to happen at odd times, since Uri was continuing his career of shows and public demonstrations, albeit at nothing like the frequency of the year before.

Again, the experiments started with what now passed for 'routine' stuff, Uri accurately picking up three-digit numbers from Puharich's mind from another room, and Uri moving a compass needle through 90 degrees; this latter, Puharich was intrigued to note, worked better when Uri put rubber bands tightly round his left hand as a tourniquet to block the return of blood from his hand. Maybe that was why the compass moving seemed to exhaust Geller. He complained to Puharich that he found it much less strenuous if he had a crowd of people around him, on whose energy he felt he could draw.

One result that fascinated Puharich was Uri's ability to bend a thin stream of water from a tap with his hand held a few centimetres away. This, he commented in his notes, was easily done by anyone with an electrically charged piece of plastic, such as a comb, but with a finger, such an effect was unheard of. The electrical charge on Uri's skin seemed to disappear when it was wet. Another simple test Puharich devised was to see whether Uri could direct a beam of energy narrowly, or whether he produced a random, scattergun effect. He laid out five matchsticks in a long row, on a glass plate monitored by a film camera. Uri was able to move whichever matchstick he chose up to 32 millimetres.

At one stage, Isaac Bentov came to join in the tests with two old friends who had been students at the Technion together in the 1940s. With four researchers poring over Uri together, Puharich noticed that Uri was starting to get bored, and the two had a 'where do we go now?' discussion with Bentov and his friends as an audience. Uri was quite clear about the nature of his problem with scientific work. Despite the advice of Amnon Rubinstein, he simply still could not see the point of it. He elaborated eloquently about how nothing mattered to him so much as he was making money, and the freedom that went with that. His life, as he saw it, had been a constant struggle to assert his freedom, with money being the ultimate way to achieve it. When the chance came to show off his powers, with his increasing love of performance, and to make money at the same time, he grabbed it. 'I want to be known. I want to be successful. If you want to work with me, you will have to deal with my need for fame and fortune. That's it,' he concluded to Puharich.

Puharich and Bentov were saddened by what they saw as the small-mindedness of this 'unabashed egomaniac', as Puharich described Geller. They all went out for dinner. On the way home, late at night, Uri insisted on giving a display of blindfold driving. This did not impress Puharich much – he knew it was an old magician's trick and how it was done, even so, was surprised by how accurately Uri managed to drive, at up to 80kph for three kilometres. He was even more surprised when Uri said he could see a red Peugeot coming, and a few moments later a red Peugeot appeared from round a bend ahead. Back at the apartment, Bentov started a late-night conversation about the soul, and how he believed Uri's was so much more evolved than other people's, but that it had become coarsened by poverty and struggle. He did not have to be so selfish and financially obsessed, Bentov said.

Uri seemed mildly interested and asked how he could find out about his soul; Puharich leapt at this and offered to hypnotize Geller. Uri was reluctant at first, but Puharich was already compiling ever more detailed notes with a view to writing a book on his Uri Geller experiences and was keen on the idea. He convinced Uri that hypnotism would be the best way to go back to his childhood and recall vital material he had forgotten, maybe explore the incident in the Arabic garden. Uri said he knew about hypnotism, being in show business, and that although he believed himself to be un-hypnotizable, he would happily give it a try.

As the guests left Puharich's apartment, one of Bentov's friends took Puharich to one side and said, 'You know, we have a word in Hebrew for a kid like Uri – *puscht*, a punk. He really is insufferable. I don't know how you can be so patient with him.' Puharich says that he replied, 'I feel he is so extraordinary that he is worth almost any effort.'

On 30 November, Uri was performing at a discotheque in Herzliya. Puharich and Bentov were planning the first hypnosis session with Geller that night, and went to see him at the louder-than-loud event. Puharich later reported being so depressed by the tawdriness of the show, just as he had been by the cabaret Uri was in at Zorba back in August, that he almost wondered if he wanted to continue with the Geller experiment any longer. Uri nevertheless turned up at Puharich's apartment with his young girlfriend, Iris, a model, and lay down on the living-room sofa just after midnight. Puharich asked him to count backwards from 25, and was pleased to note that by the time he got to 18, Geller was in a deep trance. He would remain in it for an hour and a half.

Both Puharich's and Uri's accounts of what happened over the forthcoming weeks almost need to come with a mental health warning; what follows certainly requires a great deal of forbearance on behalf of the reader. While reading this material, and more likely than not scoffing at it, it is important, however, constantly to bear in mind one or two things.

Firstly, that Uri, while still being rather embarrassed by his and his then-mentor's accounts of events, does not attempt to deny or suppress them, but rather to attempt to explain, which is far from an easy job. The obvious conclusion is that he was extravagantly conned by Puharich. Yet if Geller stands accused of one thing by his detractors, it is of being a cunning deceiver – not of being gullible or impressionable himself.

Secondly, Puharich was many things, but not a rogue or a charlatan, at least according to those who knew him, and in many cases clashed with him. One can only ask the reader to keep this in mind for the next few moments.

Once Uri was fully under the hypnotic trance on the sofa in the Herzliya apartment, Puharich asked him where he was. Geller talked initially about being in the caves back in Cyprus, with Joker, his dog. 'I come here for learning,' Uri said. 'I just sit here in the dark with Joker. I learn and learn, but I don't know who is doing the teaching.' Puharich asked what he was learning. Geller replied that it was a secret, about people who come from space, and that he would tell Puharich all about them, but not yet. Uri then lapsed into Hebrew, with Bentov doing a running translation. After telling of many trivial childhood incidents, he finally talked about the light in the Arabic garden opposite his parents' flat in Tel Aviv.

He named the day it happened as 25 December 1949, a date that obviously has some resonance, although not, it must be noted, in Israel, of course, where Christmas Day is just another working day. Uri described the light he saw in the garden as a large, shining bowl, from which a figure appeared, faceless but exuding what Uri said was 'a general radiance'. Then the figure raised its arms and held them above its head, so it appeared to be holding the sun. It then became so bright that Uri passed out.

At this point, according to Puharich, a mechanical, robotic voice was heard in the apartment, either coming from Uri or directly above him. The voice spoke for a couple of minutes, after which Puharich ended the session and woke Uri. Puharich told him about the strange voice, which Uri clearly did not believe. Puharich played him the section of the tape leading up to the voice's intervention, where Uri's voice could be heard describing what had happened in the garden. This made Uri frightened and agitated, as he did not remember any of the long session under hypnosis.

As soon as the tape reached the mechanical voice part, Puharich reported, Uri swiftly ejected it, took it in his left hand, and closed his fist over the cassette, whereupon it vanished. He then rushed out of the apartment and ran away. Puharich, Bentov and Iris searched everywhere, worried that he might still be in a partial trance and could hurt himself. After half an hour, they found him, as Puharich put it, 'like a standing mummy'. They took him back into the apartment, and decided that he needed to go home and sleep. Iris agreed to take him home, while Puharich and Bentov decided to reconstruct all they could recall of the strange voice's words while the memory was still fresh.

Their reconstruction ran thus: *'It was us who found Uri in the garden when he was three. We programmed him in the garden for many years to come, but he was also programmed not to remember. On this day, our work begins. Andrija, you are to take care of him. We reveal ourselves because we believe that man may be on the threshold of a world war. Plans for war have been made by Egypt, and if Israel loses, the entire world will explode into war. There will be one last round of negotiations that may not avert war. America is the problem. The negotiations will not succeed. The Egyptians have as of now no fixed date to start the war. The critical dates as seen by us are 12, 15, 20, 25, 26 December 1971– or nothing at all.'*

Puharich and Bentov stayed up all night, as one might imagine, discussing what they were dealing with. The following day, Puharich was alone in the apartment, catching up on his sleep, when Uri arrived in Herzliya, seeming, Puharich reported, unusually relaxed. Puharich had earlier placed a specially machined steel ring, made by Bentov in his workshop, into a wooden microscope box. Why he had put it in the box, Puharich was not sure; maybe he had planned to get Uri to bend it. But Uri suddenly asked, 'Why did you put the ring in the box?' Puharich said he didn't know. Uri then demanded that Puharich get out the movie camera, take a film of him putting the ring in the box, and he would then make the ring disappear. After Puharich had done as he'd been told to, Uri placed his hands over the box for around two minutes then told him to check the box. The ring had vanished. 'This was,' Puharich wrote later, 'the first time I had experienced an object vanishing where I was certain there was no deception involved.'

Another day, Puharich took a brass, ink-refill cartridge with the number #347299 on it, put it inside a ballpoint pen, then put the pen in a wooden box, all in an attempt to produce a variation on the disappearing-ring phenomenon. After Uri had held his hands over the box, the pen stayed put, but the cartridge had vanished. A few days later, on 9 December, Uri felt an urge to go to a certain point in a suburb east of Tel Aviv at night. He drove out with Puharich and Iris, and there, above a building site, the three of them saw a bluish, pulsating light. Uri felt drawn to the light and told the others to stay by the car. As he approached, he saw a massive object and, in a near-trance, sensed he was being drawn into its interior. When he went inside, he believed he could make out control panels. Then a dark shape approached him and put something in his hand. Seconds later he was outside again, and running up to Puharich and Iris. Puharich checked what

Uri was holding in his hand. It was a brass, ballpoint ink-refill cartridge with the number #347299 engraved on it.

Puharich's Sony tape recorder continued to issue its communiqués, summoning Uri to witness UFO fly-pasts, teleportations and other phenomena. Yet every tape made of the voice disappeared. Puharich believed Uri was relaying messages from The Nine. Sometimes the voice would come out of Puharich's recorder in the same monotonous, automated tone. The mysterious aliens, from a world called Hoova, and sometimes calling themselves Rhombus 4D, had assigned Puharich and Geller a variety of tasks, which would test their faith and abilities. The Nine had given the pair a central role in preventing war, as well as making them foot soldiers in a grand design for Earth, which they admitted was principally for their own needs and benefit, but which would, at the same time, be the greatest thing mankind had ever experienced. They reassured Puharich, through Uri, that they had been directing his, Puharich's, life and career for decades, as well as Uri's. They explained that their city-sized spacecraft, called Spectra, was responsible for Uri's odd powers, and the way mankind received Uri Geller would determine whether and how Hoova's Earth-development programme would continue, as well as the planet's general fate. For some subtle, cosmic reason, Uri was deliberately being sent into the world under the cover of a clownish, comic act.

Possible interpretations of this flood tide of what most people would dismiss as wild fantasy are unlimited. Maybe it was just a weird symbiosis between Uri's and Puharich's fertile imaginations, each sparking the other off in an atmosphere of increasing hysteria. Puharich became utterly obsessed with his watch, whose wild, erratic hand movements in Uri's presence were for him the everyday calling card of The Nine. The two men also, said Puharich, experienced extraordinary teleportations almost daily. On one such occasion they have both reported, an electrical massage machine Puharich had left in New York and which Uri had expressed a desire to use, appeared in its box in working order in the Herzliya apartment. There were dozens more such incidents. Puharich continued to log every minuscule detail for his extraordinary 1974 book, *Uri*, a work that, page by curiously unreadable page, became less credible and more damaging and discomforting to its subject.

Uri is only too aware today that such stories do little to help his cause. While the terrifying craziness that later took place at the Lawrence Livermore Laboratory has plenty of living witnesses to attest to it, these events in Israel were related only by a long-dead eccentric and, with appropriate caveats by the bucket load, by Uri. For once, Shipi was not present. 'Maybe,' he says today, 'these apparent teleportations and the voices from the tape recorder were part of a deep, elaborate hoax by Andrija to get me into his clutches? Perhaps he packed the massage machine in a suitcase and shipped it to Tel Aviv just in case I mentioned it and he could impress me by being like a genie who could make a trivial wish of mine just appear?'

To take Andrija Puharich intellectually apart is almost too easy; yet to dismiss him as a madman is too simplistic; he *was* a real scientist; he did, with great success, deliver Geller to a worldwide scientific audience. Most of his notes have a ring of plodding accuracy about them, whether they reflect objective truth or not. Indigestible as *Uri* was, Puharich was not at all a relentlessly earnest man, or, as we have seen by his taking his *Perry Mason* cameo role, one without humour. He was not lacking in worldly wiles either; he orchestrated getting Uri on to every TV talk show in the USA.

'Was it a mistake for Geller to link up with Puharich?' pondered John Hasted, an atomic physicist, and retired Professor of Experimental Physics, at Birkbeck College, University of London, who, before his death in 2002, worked with Uri after he came to the UK in 1974. 'No, it wasn't,' he continued, at his home in Cornwall. 'No one else could have got other people interested. Puharich was a medical electronics man, a reputable electroengineer. He was also very personable but not absurdly so, and a very *nice* man.'

To get a final firm fix on Puharich at this stage in the Uri Geller story, we need to spin forward a couple of years in the narrative. Puharich had bought – using whose funds, it is not known – a magnificent 15-room house with six acres, a brook and a pond at 87 Hawkes Avenue, Ossining, New York. This became his base for what was, at his Uri Geller apogee, a virtual Puharich cult. The Puharich place was known in Ossining as a hangout for oddballs, otherwise 'The Turkey Farm' or 'Lab Nine'.

Uri's attitude to Puharich over this bizarre period in Israel is best characterized as that of a favoured nephew defending an eccentric, erratic but brilliant uncle, to whom he owes a great deal, and with whom he had a special intellectual connection. He declines to dissociate himself entirely from Puharich's wilder theories. He appreciated Andrija's approach from the outset. 'Here he was, this good-looking Einstein, full of joy and fascination and interest. There was something about him that to me said, this is an important man that I have to listen to. He was almost like a guide to me.' Liking

Puharich was one thing, but most important for Uri was that he was prepared to accept as reality his childhood Joan-of-Arc vision – and to run with it.

While the rest of the world was still struggling with trying to believe or not believe in Geller's powers, one could take the view that Puharich was managing to get Uri Geller to believe in an Uri Geller of his, Puharich's, most idealized imaginings: exit Svengali, enter Dr Frankenstein. The vision in the garden and the ensuing feeling of 'differentness' that this had engendered in Uri as a boy was the ideal starting point for Puharich to gain Geller's compliance in the construction of a new version of himself as a higher being. The extent of Geller's affirmation of this idea of himself has varied over the years.

'Such bizarre things started happening when Andrija came into my life,' Uri attests, 'like the incident with the massage machine. I wanted one so badly, and suddenly, it materializes from New York to Israel. I wake up and there is a massage machine in front of my bed. When this kind of thing happens, you either think you are totally out of it, or you have to accept them, because it is a fact. I questioned his credibility, I believed he had brainwashed me. I don't question my own sanity. I had gone through a war and gone through Cyprus, crazy things had happened since childhood. I read minds.

'I think there are no in-betweens here. It's either, I really saw what I saw and it was there in physical form, or not. But then many a time the idea sneaked up on me that maybe he managed to hypnotize me to such an extent that he actually implanted these ideas and images into my mind. So when, for instance, we saw a huge disc in the Sinai desert, perhaps it was really my imagination and it wasn't there. Then there were other times when I thought he had sprinkled my food and drink with magic mushrooms, on which he happened to be an expert. Or he had turned me into a zombie.

'Then again, my relationship with Puharich was a very long one, and you can't poison food every time you plan for Uri Geller to see something. And, yes, there is supposed to be a phenomenon where your mind or your subconscious can put itself on magnetic tape. Maybe Andrija found a way either by hypnotism or by triggering some ability in me to create those tapes. But then the voices I heard *were* very real. So it was seeing, hearing and smelling, and as far as I feel, it was a fact I saw these things.

'But did I really see these things? You must understand,' Geller continues, 'because we were in this situation, it looked quite normal to me in a way. Yes it was bizarre, bordering on insane. To the outside person, who was not involved, it looked like total madness and hysteria. But it seemed normal. From the day I met Andrija, he was very accurate. He kept diaries. He was 100 per cent sure that an extraterrestrial intelligence was working through me, using me as a vehicle for it to achieve certain things here. There was some sort of code system through his watch. OK, in a very strange way, I disconnected myself from that scene while it was going on. I let things happen. The UFO in the Sinai, and the one I saw with Puharich and Iris and in the suburbs of Tel Aviv, they were all happening to me, and I took it very naturally, just said to myself, let it happen.

'When he hypnotized me, some of the voices came through me, but I was awake when I heard the words come out of the tape recorder. Did I hallucinate? No way. But because of the way the tapes in the machine dematerialized every time they should have been recording the voice from Spectra, I suspected Andrija, because he had come with the tape recorder. Once, when he wasn't in the room, I opened it with a screwdriver, just to satisfy myself that this wasn't a trick tape recorder that could gulp down a tape and make it disappear. Yes, then I thought Andrija was tricking me. He was totally immersed in me, Uri Geller, for no monetary reason. I had to tell him that if he wanted me out of Israel, I wanted to buy my mother an apartment before I left. He actually loaned me money with which I bought my mother an apartment. It was new for me to see such a non-financial motivation.

'Now when Andrija's book came out and I was being interviewed, I was very supportive to him. I had to go along with his idea, because I was a believer, because he painted the canvas and I interpreted it from the canvas. Now, in the modern world, having studied how radicalization of terrorists takes place, I wonder whether he was using his psychological skills and ability with hypnotism to radicalize me towards this insane belief system? But when I parted ways with Andrija years later, if I had disputed what he had written, it would mean that I was just some kind of conspirator, and I lied. But because I still very deeply believe that what was occurring between me and Andrija was real, I couldn't brush it aside.

'If you look at an interview in its entirety, I would go on about 90 per cent about my powers and abilities and that would give a little opening of about ten per cent to the possibility that these voices were some kind of an extraterrestrial intelligence. I never said that this was a hoax from Andrija or that it wasn't real, or that this was his imagination. I said it exactly as it happened. What can I do when Andrija opens a Sony tape, a new one, in front of my very own eyes, tears off the Cellophane, puts it into the tape recorder, presses the button to record and a mechanical voice comes on?

'This is the big difference between me and many other paranormalists. They think that paranormal powers come from within you, whereas I say that's possible, but I believe that in my case, it could just possibly be coming from outside, from a thinking entity, and that it is the entity which decides what to do. The fact is that here I am after all these years, and I am still in contact with something. If that's controversial to some closed-minded people, fuck them. The fact is that these occurrences are still continuing to happen to me – and not only to me.'

As Uri's American adventure came closer in the first part of 1972, and all the scientific testing and contact with the intelligence and military detailed in earlier chapters were still to come, he and Shipi first headed for Germany, where an Israeli impresario, Yasha Katz, was sure he had spotted an opportunity for some lucrative TV and theatre work. Barely 25 years after the Holocaust, West Germany was especially welcoming to Israelis; to decent people ashamed of its recent Nazi past, the young country had acquired something approaching hero status. Uri also had a secondary, secret reason for wanting to be in Munich in the early summer of 1972. His Mossad contact, with the knowledge of Aharon Yariv from Israeli Military Intelligence, too, wanted him to sniff around the Olympic Park where the games were soon to be held and see if he could sense anything foreboding. As we learned earlier, Uri certainly was not happy about the site and recommended that the Israeli team did not travel. They did, and in the massacre that followed 11 Israeli athletes and coaches and a West German policeman were killed (as were five of those responsible for the attack).

As things also turned out, from the point of view of entertainment shows, Germany was not as big a hit as Katz believed it would be. But for media publicity above and beyond anything possible in the village that was Israel, Germany was a great dry run for America, and later for the UK. Not only that: Uri's 1972 trip to Germany also put him in front of more scientists.

Uri's experience abroad was minimal, however. He had tried performing in Italy with limited success, and was distinctly nervous about going straight to the States and submitting himself to the scrutiny of scientists who might be a good deal less friendly than Puharich or Meir Gitlis. Uri and Shipi were seen off by an odd party of well-wishers, consisting of his divorced parents, Shipi's parents, Hanna – and Iris. Shipi, now a smart 17-year-old, had left school, but still had some time to go before he was required for his army service so was now Uri's fully fledged personal and road manager as well as, to all intents, his kid brother.

The young men went first to Rome, which Uri was familiar with and where they spent a few days in an apartment lent by a friend. Uri rented a car and he and Shipi took a leisurely drive north, stopping off in St. Moritz, where they met two Australian girls they spent some time with. Devouring the mountain scenery, the luxury and wealth all around them, almost unimaginable compared to what they were used to in Israel, they continued to Munich, where Yasha Katz was waiting for them, a friendly-looking man of nearly 40, Uri observed, with a crinkly face. Uri liked him immediately. Katz had an entire show tour already planned, but more importantly, he introduced Uri to friendly tabloid newspaper coverage.

In Israel, the popular newspapers were always a little prickly about Uri, not necessarily in the good sense of being cautiously sceptical. There is, as so many Israelis point out, a jealous streak in their national culture that manifests itself in many people as a desire to be spiteful at worst, sarcastic at best, about anyone who achieves success. Geller fell foul of this, and as part of the same syndrome, of the perils of what might be called the instant-expert, black-and-white school of journalism. This is the type of reportage that depends on academics – almost any academic with a halfway, decent-looking qualification will do – ready at the end of a telephone to come up with a derogatory, off-the-cuff comment about something or someone, which is reported as expert opinion, and often comes to count as such.

In Germany, Uri Geller hit on the other side of the same coin – newspapers that saw him as good news, and would not naïvely assume that because one scientist dismissed him as a fraud, all others would all do the same. In Uri Geller, the Munich newspaper *Bild Zeitung*, the first in Germany to go big on him, found a fascinating story of the paranormal personified in a character of a tabloid editor's dreams – young, handsome, heterosexual, earnest, articulate and even from a favoured country – Israel being all the more favoured after the terrorist massacre of several of the country's athletes at the Munich Olympics, an outrage that occurred while Geller was living in the city.

Bild Zeitung went ahead with a six-part Uri Geller series, and even managed to get some informal scientific backup for him from a serious physicist. He stopped a cable car, bent the Mayor of Munich's wedding ring and, later, a set of handcuffs at a police station – all this after he had been, with his agreement, strip-searched for any illicit conjuring aids. Then *Bild Zeitung* took Geller along for an informal meeting in a hotel with a 32-year-old physicist who worked at the Max Planck Institute for Plasma Physics at Garching, just outside Munich.

Although he was more mainstream than Andrija Puharich, Dr Friedbert Karger, it is fair to say, was still not quite an everyday physicist. A specialist in thermonuclear fusion – the study of hot temperatures – he had also studied psychology and philosophy, and spent much of his professional life examining paraphysics, especially poltergeist and other psychokinetic phenomena, alongside his conventional work at the Institute. He was a natural for *Bild Zeitung* to ask to do a preliminary assessment of Uri Geller.

Karger came prepared with a ring, which he handled cautiously, never taking his eyes off it or letting it leave his hand. Uri touched it gently in Karger's palm and concentrated on it. The ring rapidly bent out of shape and cracked in two places. A colleague from the Institute, Manfred Lipa, also examined the ring for tool marks and found none. Karger also brought a diving watch, which Geller altered without any detectable trickery. Journalists asked Karger if the damage to the ring could have been caused by strong pressure. He said it could not. By a laser? 'No!' Karger replied. The only other possibility was that Geller had tried some form of hypnosis, but he considered that unlikely.

Karger summed up: 'The powers of this man are a phenomenon that in theoretical physics cannot be explained. It is like atomic science. At the turn of the century, it was already known as a reality. It was just that at that time, one could not yet explain it in terms of physics.' ('Naturally,'

Karger reflected many years later, 'some of my colleagues said the usual thing, that he was doing good tricks and nothing else. But they had not done experiments with him, and I had. I think he has both psychokinetic and telepathic abilities.')

When asked what the physical mechanism might be to explain how Uri's effects work, Karger preferred not to speculate – but hinted that the Uri Geller effect, poltergeist effects, and even stranger paranormal anomalies might all be one and the same. 'Many very well-known physicists have done this work, you know,' he told the author. 'Einstein investigated spiritualist mediums, and Pauli and other Nobel Prize winners did similar experiments. If you are ignorant of these phenomena, it's easy to dismiss them, but if you have seen the phenomena you have to ask the questions I have.'

But the summer idyll in Germany, with a friendly media and supportive scientists, could not last forever. It was ruined by the September massacre of the Israeli athletes almost under Uri and Shipi's nose and with the knowledge in their minds that Uri had warned against something bad happening. Puharich and Edgar Mitchell were also urging Uri daily to get on a flight to the States and start seeing the line-up of interested scientists – and impatient CIA people – they had contacted.

The laboratory testing, the flirting with intelligence and military work, the global publicity that stemmed from Puharich finally getting Uri to America, we now know about. But some of the offstage happenings around Uri are also extraordinary and noteworthy – none more so than what occurred on a freezing, early Friday evening in November 1973, when Uri was staying in New York at his seventh-floor apartment on 57th and 1st. This particular night, Uri walked to the apartment where his friends Byron and Maria Janis lived. There, he had made a couple of phone calls, one to Puharich in Ossining, 58 kilometres north of New York City. At this stage, Uri's relationship with the ever more possessive Puharich was tense and fractured, but still more or less intact.

After Uri had made his calls, Byron remembers, he said he had to go to Bloomingdale's to buy something, and had some other things to do around Manhattan. 'He was very excited,' Janis says. 'I assumed it was to do with a woman. He liked women very much.' At 5.30, Maria Janis says, referring to notes she made later that night, Uri left the apartment. Bloomingdale's was eight minutes' walk away, Uri's own apartment, two minutes in the opposite direction. The round trip to the store, into the camera department (where he bought a pair of binoculars) and home would have taken 20 minutes. Maria knows this because she has paced the journey out repeatedly in an effort to explain what then happened, because Uri never reached home. Twenty-five minutes after he left, the phone went. Maria took it, and Byron happened to pick up the extension. It was Andrija Puharich, calling from Ossining. 'There's someone here who wants to talk to you,' Puharich said gravely.

'Then,' Byron says, 'Uri came on the line. He said, "Maria, I'm here." He was obviously in shock. She said, "Uri, what are you doing there?" I thought it was a joke. But it was obvious that somehow, Uri had got to Ossining, and it was clear that he was a complete wreck. He went through the story on the phone. He said as he got to the canopy in front of his building, "I felt this sudden pull backwards and up." Those were his exact words. "And the next thing I knew, I was falling through the screen door in Ossining."' It seemed unlikely to the Janises that this could have been a stunt, even if they thought Uri capable of pulling one, or had the remotest need to impress them, of all people, who completely trusted Uri's authenticity. Yet they considered everything; a train or car getaway to Ossining was impossible in 25 minutes, especially on a busy, winter Friday rush hour. Even a split second-timed helicopter operation would have taken longer, because of the time it would have taken to get to a helipad in central Manhattan.

Puharich, in an unpublished account found by his children after his death, confirmed the Janises' chronology. In his meticulous detail-noting style, he recounted having been watching the six o'clock news on television while lying on his bed – the main story was of Henry Kissinger's shuttle diplomacy between Israel and Egypt – and felt a shudder with a simultaneous crash from, as it turned out, a conservatory he used in the summer as a dining room. He also heard the faint voice of Uri calling his name. When he found Uri, he appeared to have fallen through the thin mesh, insect-protective roof of the conservatory, rather than come in through the screen door. He had landed, hands first, on a round, wooden coffee table, whose glass top had slipped off and shattered on the floor. He was unhurt, but clearly confused and dazed. And he was carrying a Bloomingdale's bag.

Uri himself recalls that the sidewalk wasn't crowded when he left the Janises' apartment. 'The first recollection I have is of me looking at the ground and seeing myself a few inches above it. The next thing I can remember is like someone had cut out a split second piece of my life, like a piece of film taken out with scissors. I remember the lifting off, then I recollect there being a screen in front of me, and putting my arms up to protect my face, as my instinct told me that I was about to crash into something. Then my palms were crashing through the screen, but ever so gently, then there I was falling on the round table, and a glass tabletop slipping from under my hands, and breaking on the floor, and me falling on the table and onto the floor. I didn't know where I was. I didn't recognize it as Andrija's porch at first, until I got my bearings. I had had many breakfasts there on that porch.'

Geller, like the Janises and Puharich, spent many months trying to puzzle out what happened that evening. 'It's beyond my understanding and comprehension to believe that my body was disintegrated molecule by molecule and reconstructed itself 58 kilometres out of New York. My explanation is that people, animals and objects can fall into a time warp, like a whirlpool of time, space and matter,' says Uri. 'You are sucked into some kind of void, a vacuum, an emptiness that could move you in space and time and replant you elsewhere.

'I could have gone back into the past or the future. Hundreds of people and children go missing each year without a trace. I'm not saying they fall into time warps or are abducted by UFOs, but no one knows where they disappear to. Maybe what is happening is that there are velocities and speeds in the universe and in our bodies and in our minds, and most likely, everything is happening right now. The past is now, the present is now and the future is now, and somehow we are just stuck in it where we are. It is like a mixture of speeds we don't understand, so what happened to me is that because my mind, my subconscious, or even deeper than that, was so concerned about my relationship with Andrija and how I wanted to tear away from him at that time, that it just pushed me into this vortex of some kind, and I teleported there.

Perhaps it was him wanting me to be back there. There were times, you know, when I began to doubt whether Andrija was human.'

On a visit to Uri in New York, Yasha Katz, who moved to South Africa and has since died, experienced some odd events, too, although nothing to compete with the Ossining incident. 'One Sunday morning a whole series of things happened in quick succession,' Katz said. 'I went to get a newspaper, and when I came back, I saw my plant holder, which was a very, very heavy glass thing, which one person could not lift, in front of the elevator door. I thought maybe Uri played a joke on me, and I went into the apartment and he wasn't in.

'He was in his apartment in the same building, so I phoned him, and he came up and said he didn't do anything. We both had to lift it and put it back in the bedroom, and as we came out from the bedroom, the lamp that was in the lounge started rattling and moving, I had a little marble frog in my bedroom, and all of a sudden, it fell through the wall from my bedroom into the main room. It actually went through the wall. I saw it do so. Then a chair that was in the lounge turned around and fell in front of us, and Uri started not so much panicking, but he was a little concerned. He said, "Yasha, I have to write this down, can you get me a Coke." And I went into the fridge, and as we opened it, a pencil came out of the can.

'Another time, we went to a gala opening on Broadway for a show called *Via Galactica*. We were sitting there, and Shipi, myself and another Israeli friend of ours were next to Uri. I noticed that there was no arm between our two chairs, and Uri didn't feel very comfortable, so I put my jacket down, and he put his arm on it. We went out and it was pouring with rain and our car was parked in a garage. While I got it, they went into a telephone booth to keep out of the rain. On the way to collect the car, I saw something floating in the air – floating, not falling. It slowly dropped down. I picked it up and I saw it was the arm of the theatre chair. I still have it. The funny thing was that, although it landed in a puddle, it was completely dry.'

Chapter Eight

LONDON CALLING

Coming for the first time to Britain in November 1973 and appearing with consummate success on a television chat show hosted by David Dimbleby was the beginning of Uri Geller's journey to what would become home. He had been brought up on stories of his father's exploits in the British Army, before he became an Israeli soldier, and he, Uri, had enjoyed a traditional British education to the equivalent of today's GCSE level in Cyprus. A decade later, he would settle in Britain, where he has now lived for over 30 years.

At times, the live Dimbleby show looked as if it would be a damp squib, like a famously abortive Johnny Carson TV appearance Uri would later make in the States. On the Dimbleby show, it took an agonizingly long period of silence, with Uri concentring hard but nothing at all happening, before things started to work in the studio – and a Geller furore was unleashed in Britain.

The reason for the uproar and excitement was that Uri had, in one jump and without having specifically planned to do so, taken his unique form of psychic entertainment-cum-education to a whole new level. He was the first person to demonstrate a scientific (or paranormal) effect – what we would now call 'interactively' – with the public at home being asked to find broken and stopped watches and clocks as well as ordinary spoons, to see if the timepieces started and the spoons bent. In this, and subsequent TV demonstrations, tens of thousands of people reported strange happenings in their own homes, and TV stations' switchboards becoming jammed with callers became the norm. (Today it would be a Twitter storm, of course.)

The Dimbleby show was a most important event for Uri, both in that it opened Britain up to him, and it helped him develop a new perspective on what it was he was actually doing. 'What you can't take away,' he says, 'is, let's say 10,000 phone calls come in to a TV show from people saying their spoons bent or their watches restarted or something else strange happened. And let's imagine that 50 per cent of them were lying. And let's say half of the remaining 5,000 imagined it. What I want to know, and what I've wondered all these years, is what about the rest? What about the other 2,500, or the 1,000, or the 500 or the 50 that weren't imagining and weren't lying or self-deluding? How does it work for them? I honestly don't know, I don't really think I want to know, and I'm not sure the Universe wants us to know. I don't believe we're ready for it.'

The new idea he formed as a result of the Dimbleby phenomenon, which was repeated regularly on shows in other countries, was that he was not the person affecting the metal, he was an enabler. 'I thought I was doing it by staring into the camera, but it wasn't that. Later, an American psychologist interested in Uri, Professor Thelma Moss of the Neuropsychiatric Institute at the University of California, Los Angeles, called him to say she had managed to get students to start stalled watches and so on by watching a video of him. The idea that even a recording of him could work as a catalyst to unleash something everyone has was a matter of some concern to Uri; if anyone could do this, wasn't he going to put himself out of a job before long?

Probably the most ringing endorsement of Uri in the immediate aftermath of his appearance on the Dimbleby show was that of the science writer Brian Silcock of *The Sunday Times*, who in the next edition of the newspaper, described an encounter with Geller in a taxi as, 'leaving this initially highly sceptical science correspondent with his mind totally blown.' Geller had caused Silcock's thick office key to bend in the flat belonging to photographer Bryan Wharton, who was holding it in his hand. He also made a paperknife bend, and Silcock and Wharton both saw it go on bending.

'It is utterly impossible to remain sceptical after seeing Uri Geller in action,' Silcock wrote, adding, 'I am convinced that Geller is a telepath too,' after Uri had reproduced pictures that the journalist was only thinking of, but had not drawn. (Over the years that followed, Silcock semi-reversed his opinion. 'I became convinced in my own mind that it was just a conjuring trick,' he told the author. 'I have no idea how the trick was done, but I think there was a process of my natural scepticism reasserting itself. I tend to be of a rather sceptical, downbeat frame of mind, and I somehow got shoved out of it. I don't really understand how that happened, either.')

Perhaps the difference between failure on NBC's Johnny Carson Show and success on the BBC's Dimbleby show can be put down to the different attitudes of the two hosts. Carson was a devout sceptic, who, it is claimed, had got the Geller-obsessed magician James Randi to rig the studio against any possibility of Uri cheating. Dimbleby (now one of Britain's senior political commentators), although a sceptic, had been quite shaken before the show to see a key he was holding bend under Geller's gaze, and once the cameras were on, he was clearly in an encouraging, positive frame of mind.

Also present on the BBC show as a scientific sceptic was John Taylor, an expert in black holes, who was Professor of Applied Mathematics at London's, King's College, and previously a Professor of Physics at Rutgers University, New Jersey. The writer on anomalous science, Lyall Watson, (author of *Supernature*) was also on hand to explain that he had wasted his first experience of Geller by looking all around him for the catch. There were, Watson pronounced, no tricks involved with Uri.

Uri was his usual engaging self, and said although he was convinced that his abilities were caused by some 'outside power', what he did might equally be powered by the people around him. He went on to do a successful telepathy test, which drew gasps from the audience, and to wreak havoc with some BBC canteen cutlery. He also caused the hands on Watson's watch to bend under the glass while he was still wearing it, an effect Uri had not seen since he was a schoolboy.

Today, Dimbleby still clearly recalls the show as a huge success, and explains his view on Geller today – as well as possibly the view of much of the British intelligentsia – with characteristic crispness. 'I saw him doing the metal bending several times with Yale keys, and I can only say what I saw,' Dimbleby says. 'He would take a key and rub it between his first finger and thumb, then put it down and hold his hand over it, and it sort of lifted up towards his hand. I saw it lift up. Once it snapped and once it was just completely bent in half. I am very pragmatic about these things I don't know what the rubbing consisted of and what happened during that process.

'The conjurer who rubbished him on telly afterwards, Paul Daniels, [today a good friend of Uri] said everyone had been conned and it was just sleight of hand,' Dimbleby added, 'But it was clear to me that what wasn't sleight of hand was that the key was on a table or in the palm of his hand, or sometimes being held by the person who had proffered it. I certainly saw the key moving without his actually touching it two or three times. He did telepathy on the programme quite impressively, and I have never seen anyone simulate properly the key bending or forks drooping and seeming to melt in his hand.'

Professor Taylor was entranced by what he saw in the BBC studio; 'I believe this process. I believe that you actually broke the fork here and now,' he said on the show, in a mixture of delight and bafflement. He took Uri off for testing at King's College, and became an enthusiastic Geller supporter. One scientific colleague recalls Taylor having in his eyes the obvious gleam of someone who could see himself getting a Nobel Prize for discovering a new scientific principle that would explain Uri Geller's abilities.

Taylor wrote a popular book, *Superminds: An Enquiry into the Paranormal,* largely about Geller and dozens of children – known as mini-Gellers – who were discovered in Britain after the Dimbleby show to have similar metal-bending abilities. For a few years, the names Taylor and Geller were almost uttered in one breath in the country. But then Taylor underwent a change of mind on Uri and the entire paranormal field. He published another book in 1980, *Science and the Supernatural*, a sort of antimatter version of *Superminds*, in which he concluded that the evidence for paranormal spoon bending was 'suggestive but certainly not watertight.'

Far less noisily in the background, however, a perhaps rather more qualified British academic – more qualified in that he was an experimental physicist – was working intensively with Geller in his laboratory in London as well as at his home in Sunningdale, Surrey. John Hasted, who held the chair in Experimental Physics at Birkbeck College, was a most unusual scientist. As well as being a world authority on his speciality, atomic collisions, he was a lifelong lover of folk songs, was deeply involved in the London skiffle scene in the 50s and 60s, and was an early activist in the nuclear protest movement, who had gone on the Campaign for Nuclear Disarmament's first Aldermaston march in 1958. Hasted was also involved in the first pirate broadcasting in Britain, a CND operation that ran from 1958 to 1959, in which transmitters were set up on the top of buildings to put out tapes of speeches by Bertrand Russell.

Hasted retired to St Ives, Cornwall, and when the author interviewed him, he was living in a bungalow overlooking the lighthouse Virginia Woolf wrote about in her famous novel. Frail, but mentally extremely agile, Hasted was still very much into peace, as well as being an enthusiastic vegetarian and a voracious reader, devouring everything from new scientific papers to Martin Amis to classics. In the 1970s, Hasted stuck his neck out and, after exhaustive laboratory tests centring on his use of mechanical strain gauges to measure accurately the bending in metal, proclaimed Uri Geller genuine. In 1981, his book *The Metal-Benders*, almost 300 pages of scientific data, speculation and anecdote, he set out his experiences with Uri and some of the child spoon benders he found, along with his theories on the phenomenon. To the end of his life, he believed strongly in paranormal metal bending, although he regarded the work he did as a comparative failure, because he never managed to work out for certain how the phenomenon worked.

'If people say Uri Geller is a magician, they have simply failed to read the published scientific evidence,' Hasted said on a leaden, winter Cornish day, looking out across the beautiful St Ives Bay, which was shrouded in a mist that blanked out the Godrevy Island lighthouse. He explained how he had been introduced to Geller by Professor David Bohm, the renowned American-born theoretical physicist, who was interested in the links between eastern mysticism and modern physics, an interest he shared with Russell Targ and others. Bohm, a member of the top-secret Manhattan Project that developed the atomic bomb, and a friend of Einstein, was pretty well convinced that Geller was genuine. Hasted, while fascinated by, as he puts it, 'the nine-tenths of science which is unknown' had no experience of the paranormal or psychic phenomena. Even so, after meeting Geller, he was soon convinced that he was genuine.

'I never had to be concerned that I was imagining seeing spoons bend,' he explained, 'because right from the very start I insisted on instruments, quite correctly of course. [The magician] Randi came to see me at Birkbeck. He was absolutely fanatical about this, but he was not very convincing. It took me about a minute before I saw how he did it, by pre-stressing the spoon. He is back in the days of bending spoons by using force, you see, but he has never attacked my more important experiments, the ones with instruments, because he doesn't understand instruments. I don't think he could have duplicated even the first experiment in Uri's hotel when I first went with Bohm, because I brought my own key, and I had identified it by weighing it very carefully – and I didn't let Uri see it until I popped it on the table. He started to stroke it, and eventually it bent – not a lot, but it bent.

'I found these *professional* sceptics to be every bit as much a menace to scientific truth and impartial observation as the worst psychic charlatans,' the professor continued. 'They write

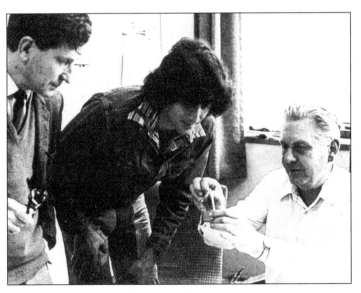

Physicist David Bohm (*left*), Uri and Professor John Hasted in England.

that researchers in the parapsychology field are emotionally committed to finding phenomena, yet forget conveniently that they themselves are emotionally committed to finding there are no phenomena. I was often reminded of a northern saying: "Them as believe nowt, will believe 'owt.'" [Which is to say, "people who refuse to believe anything are often the most gullible." Hasted was referring to the way he found that sceptics could be, ironically, convinced by the kookiest conspiracy theory if it bolsters their scepticism.]

'It was a slight shock seeing that key bend,' Hasted continued, 'but there are far worse shocks than that in science. I was just puzzled. I doubt if I would have taken it much further had not Bohm pointed out to me that if that was genuine, we were onto something very important. David Bohm's main contribution to science was the insistence on what are called non-local phenomena in quantum theory, and he was one of the great experts on quantum theory throughout the world, so I took him very seriously indeed.

Hasted, like Bohm – and also the Nobel Prize-winning, Cambridge physicist, Professor Brian Josephson – came to believe that what was happening in the case of Geller and the genuine child metal benders (some were, as might be expected, found when they were videoed secretly to be attention-seeking hoaxers) was 'a nonlocal quantum interaction'. In other words, atoms in the metal were being dislocated at a distance by some instantaneously acting force. What neither Hasted and Bohm nor Josephson could suggest was what it was in the human brain that could cause such atomic dislocations, but the theory was a starting point for some theory connecting quantum and brain functioning. 'I believe there are psychic abilities,' Professor Josephson told the author. 'They don't accord with any science we have at the moment, but maybe some future science will back them up with theories.'

The most extraordinary events during John Hasted's involvement with Uri Geller was when Hasted brought his experimental subject back from Birkbeck to his home in Sunningdale. It was there, during and after Geller's visit, that a series of poltergeist-type phenomena occurred. The first was within minutes of Uri's arrival, when Hasted observed at the back door of his kitchen, where he and his late wife, Lynn, were sitting, an ivory statuette that was normally in the sitting room appear, then fall from the ceiling to the floor. This was followed by the key of an unused antique clock that normally stood next to the statuette appearing. Over the next few weeks, there were countless instances of objects seeming to have travelled through solid walls or from inside containers, often when an increasingly frightened Lynn, who was previously dismissive about the paranormal, was on her own. The clock key kept making its own way to the identical spot by the back door, the statuette would be found on its side. Then the clock, which had no pendulum and had not worked for 30 years, started chiming, which caused Lynn to phone Hasted at the laboratory and beg him to come home. That evening, the clock – which later returned to its dead state and now took pride of place in Hasted's sitting room in Cornwall – chimed continually.

The frequency of these strange occurrences in Hasted's house increased, culminating in a particularly disturbing incident two days before Christmas. The Hasteds happened to have a good local butcher in Sunningdale, and a friend asked them if they would order his Christmas turkey for him. The friend came round to collect the bird late in the evening, the day before Christmas Eve. When the Hasteds and their friend went into the kitchen to pick the turkey up, something more than a little alarming had happened, especially for the vegetarian Hasted. It was reminiscent in its grotesque, baffling imagery to the phenomena that had so upset the nuclear physicists at the Livermore Laboratory in California a few weeks previously. The turkey's liver had apparently extricated itself from inside the still-sealed plastic bag of giblets, and rematerialized outside the untorn bag. The liver was lying in the middle of a plain white table, no trace of a blood smear near it, as would have been expected if it had moved across the surface.

With dozens of other bizarre physical phenomena happening to Hasted at work, to his colleagues and to the Hasteds' friends, the turkey incident, however, was one too many for Lynn. She threatened to leave her husband over it, although both of them suspected that it was with Lynn's unwitting cooperation that Geller had in some way let loose the avalanche of psychic. 'It was a remarkable series of incidents,' Hasted says now. 'It was a hard time for my wife and myself; we nearly fell out. We really had quite serious emotional troubles about it. I wasn't frightened; I can't become frightened by little pieces of metal; they weren't ghosts or anything like that. But she was very scared.'

While the phenomena eventually stopped, as at Livermore, and the Hasteds stayed together, the events moved Hasted's thinking on from puzzling over spoon bending to considering the wider question of teleportation. 'My attitude on this is that when metal bends, atoms move about in the metal, and if enough atoms moved around, then the whole object *could* jump, and this would be teleportation – which I now believe to be merely another branch of metal bending. In fact teleportation is probably the more fundamental event, and both Uri and some of the children I studied at the time have done it for me under very good conditions indeed. Eventually, this could be a solution of the transport problem. Yes! "Beam me up Scottie!" I think we might get there within 50 or 100 years – except that it will be very dangerous in that your head might come off or something like that. Teleportation from A to B is instantaneous, because it is another demonstration of quantum nonlocality. Nonlocality means the same thing being in two places at once, things not moving, but just appearing, going through walls. That's been my experience.'

In Hasted's cluttered study, he kept the mementoes of his pioneering metal-bending work alongside half-disembowelled bits of computers and other electronic gadgets. The bent and mangled forks and spoons were carefully marked with handmade sticky labels. Most were the product of metal benders other than Geller, and the quite grotesque distortions were greater than anything Uri produced. 'There's no doubt,' Hasted said, 'that some of the children were real mini-Gellers, and some were more powerful than Uri. I had one, whose parents were Oxford academics, who on one occasion walked through his bedroom wall in front of them. Most of these children, we found, were rather unhappy, and usually had problems with their father, and were closer to their mother – which I believe describes Uri's position.

'You will find, however, that in adulthood, they are almost all reluctant to talk about what they could do as children, or tell you whether they can still do it, some because they were cheating and are embarrassed, and others because it brings back this tortured time in their past. Uri was unusual in taking a different course, I think, because he wanted to impress, but also to be a good publicist for the cause. That was his whole end object.'

Hasted had said that he believed that in the author's lifetime, but not in his (he died in 2002), teleportation would become an established scientific effect. On the Friday of the week he said it, *Nature* published a five-page article from Professor Anton Zeilinger and other researchers at the University of Innsbruck in Austria, describing the first-ever successful verification of quantum teleportation – not quite of Scottie or of an ivory statuette or a turkey liver, but of the electrical charge on a single photon particle two metres across their laboratory. The Innsbruck team were not looking into the possibilities of mind-over-matter being a quantum effect, but suggested that theirs was the first experimental proof that quantum mechanics might soon be used to transfer information in computers infinitely faster than we can now do by mere electronics.

The *Nature* article happened to be published within days of another experiment, this one in the USA, producing the first virtually incontrovertible evidence of mind-power influencing material objects. A team at Princeton University, working under Professor Robert Jahn, the distinguished aerospace scientist, documented subjects beating odds of 1,000 billion to one when willing a random-number generator to produce specific sequences.

A few months later, there was news – some good, some bad – from Japan concerning the paranormal. The good news was that the Sony Corporation announced it had proved after seven years' research that ESP exists. The bad news was that the Corporation was closing down its ESP research facility because there did not seem to be any way to turn the knowledge into marketable products. While Uri was living with his family in Japan at one point, he had met one of Sony's founders, Masaru Ibuka, and the company's research into ESP had stemmed from this meeting. Neither the Princeton team nor the one at Sony suggested that a quantum effect was behind their respective discoveries. But at least for the first time, the possibility of an explanation for the Geller effect – that his brain and those of others can cause thoughts, atoms in metal, and entire objects to move around by a form of quantum teleportation – began to look howsoever dimly realistic.

One of the key events John Hasted organized for Geller when he was in England was an informal gathering of high-powered, interested parties in his lab at Birkbeck on a June Saturday in 1974. Among those who came to meet Geller were the chief engineer of the Rolls-Royce Rocket Division, Val Cleaver, Arthur Koestler, the engineer-turned-science writer, who later bequeathed £1m to found a chair of parapsychology at a British University that was eventually established at Edinburgh University, Arthur C. Clarke, the science fiction writer, and a third Arthur, Arthur Ellison, Professor of Electrical Engineering at City University, London and a part-time researcher into the paranormal.

The meeting became famous as the source of an ongoing argument between Clarke and several of the others. When Clarke saw his front door key bend before his eyes, according to Ellison and others present, he exclaimed, 'My God, it's *Childhood's End* come true.' (A reference to one of his own novels, in which the alien overlord Karellan explains to the human race some centuries hence that the ancient mystics had been right, and science wrong, and such phenomena as poltergeists, telepathy and precognition were real). Clarke then said to Byron Janis, Uri's classical-pianist friend, who was also present, 'My God, what is this world coming to?'

'Five or six years later,' Janis related at his apartment in Manhattan, 'Clarke said it hadn't happened at all, and that he had been in a hypnotic state. It pissed me off, because I remembered it so well.' Clarke had indeed turned rather abruptly on Geller. Ten years after the Birbeck meeting, in the forward to a fairly way-out paranormal book of his own, *Arthur C. Clarke's World of Strange Powers* – a companion to a TV series – Clarke urged his readers, a little incongruously, to study Randi's debunking of Geller and was scathing about Uri. Leaving aside the fact that the magician would be bound to dismiss the whole of Clarke's book on principle (the principle that in his world view there are no strange powers) Clarke admitted he had indeed made the comment as reported when his key bent, but said that everyone else's memory of the actual bending process, bar his own, had been at fault, and that Geller had actually manipulated the key.

Up to his death in 2000, Professor Ellison remained resolute on this matter. 'Clarke got out a Yale key and he put it on top of Hasted's secretary's typewriter,' he recalled. 'We were standing around the desk in the outer office. Clarke put his finger on the key, which was all alone on that flat surface, and said to Geller, "See what you can do with that."

'I was to one side within a foot of it, Arthur Koestler was a foot away elsewhere, and Geller came up between us and stroked it on the flat back of the typewriter. All of us were watching that key like a hawk, and the end curled up in about a minute. You could rock it to and fro. Our attention was not distracted, we weren't born yesterday, we were all aware of magicians' tricks, and there was nothing else that happened that I haven't mentioned, so there's not the slightest doubt in my mind. If I have seen something I will say so. I will not be short of the courage of admitting if I see things that the general scientists think are impossible. Clarke was amazed at the time, so I was surprised when I saw him on a TV programme that he was very non-committal about Geller. I think he probably feels that if he admits to seeing a paranormal phenomenon, everyone will assume he's going round the bend and will cease taking him seriously.'

Ellison, lived in a detached suburban house on a tree-lined avenue in Beckenham, outside London. Somehow, it was not the kind of place you would have expected to find either a world-renowned scientist, or a leading light in psychical research, yet Ellison was both. The son of a tailor from Birmingham, his background was in heavy electrical engineering, from which he went into academia in 1958. Ellison was also prominent in the Scientific and Medical Network, an international group of thousands of doctors and scientists with an interest in spiritual and paranormal matters.

'My rule has always been,' Ellison explained, 'that if ever I talk about anything paranormal in the university common room, then I make jolly sure that the evidence for its truth is about an order of magnitude stronger than anything else in normal science. The standard and the quality of the research in parapsychology is a great deal higher than it is in most subjects. I have had several sharp rows on the radio about the paranormal with people like Richard Dawkins, who is the Oxford Professor for the Public Understanding of Science, and Lewis Wolpert at the Middlesex School of Medicine.

'I have discovered the way to deal with Lewis now is to talk about quantum mechanics, the fact that a great many distinguished physicists think that what's out there depends on our consciousness for its meaning in reality. Nobody would say that the fathers of quantum mechanics, like Niels Bohr and the other distinguished members of the Copenhagen group of physicists, were idiots. Even Lewis wouldn't say that. Life just isn't as simple as people like them, who I call naïve materialists, love to believe.

'As for Geller,' Professor Ellison continued, 'I think he is important in that he shows how certain things that some normal scientists consider impossible are not impossible, but as they have been conditioned by their education and training to "normal" reality, they just dismiss it all as conjuring, so that it is not as important to them as it ought to be. If they had the truly open mind of a real scientist they would be very interested in things that don't appear to be obeying what they consider to be the normal laws of nature.'

Remarkably for a man who was a visiting professor at MIT (Massachusetts Institute of Technology) and the author of a string of papers and books on highly pragmatic matters, such as the problems of noise and vibration in electric machines, Professor Ellison (DSc Eng., CEng, FIMechE, FIEE, Sen Mem IEEE, to give him his full canonicals) went beyond even quantum theory to explain Uri Geller. 'I don't actually think it is Geller who bends the metal,' he said. 'You will no doubt be what I call a naïve realist. You think there is no doubt that all these objects are around us, and you have in your mind a model of the physical world, which usually works all right, and so do I much of the time. But I actually think there are not real objects around us, and that is the result of my own experience of the paranormal.

'I have been to every kind of séance you can imagine, I have had every kind of experience that there is within the paranormal. My boggle threshold is at infinity I think. I have seen an apport [the production of objects by apparently supernatural means at a spiritualist's séance] arrive in the middle of a séance in a good light, an object that wasn't there before, a rose, a living rose, slowly materializing. I have seen objects floating in the air in a good light. I was once in a séance when the control personality, through the medium in trance, while the light was still on, said, "Hold my hand." So I linked fingers and there was a luminous trumpet kind of painted on the carpet in the middle of a big circle of spiritualists. And I held my hands out, and this trumpet floated up in the air, went round and round our linked hands half a dozen times, before it floated back down to the carpet again. I have seen and made notes on some 30 full-scale materializations, so you'll understand that I didn't turn a hair at seeing a key bent.'

Ellison gave some weight to Uri's insistence that since the age of four or five he has had no real idea of how he does what he does. The professor believed psychicism occurs at an unconscious level, where people have no control over it, and also cannot be switched on like a tap. He also considered it sometimes occurs in people who do not expect it, when they experience what some psychiatrists term a 'temporary suspension of disbelief'.

One of many intriguing things about Ellison when he discussed Uri was that he was far from an acolyte, yet still supported him. Ellison had wanted to study Geller back in

1973, but was beaten to it by Hasted and Taylor. 'Geller did invite me out to his house, once, when, I think, he really wanted this legal document to help him, an affidavit about the Arthur C. Clarke business. He promised to invite the family to see a bit of metal bending, but he never did. He is most unreliable. I slightly suspect he sometimes tells stories that aren't quite accurate, and occasionally makes promises that he can't keep. I also can't swear that he doesn't at some times use stage magicianship. If anyone is paid as much as he is and it doesn't work one evening, I imagine it's a terrible temptation to fake it a bit, if not for the self-respect, then at least for your money – and to give them what they paid for. That showmanship thing has done quite a lot to damage the subject. But the great thing with Uri is that he can get members of the audience, with no extra grind, to bend their own keys. Now that's fantastic, and I applaud Uri for it, because it's not Uri doing it; they are doing it themselves. It's that temporary suspension of disbelief.'

Another still supportive scientist with a view on Uri that is nonetheless not wholly approving is Zvi Bentwich, an internationally eminent immunologist, director of Israel's Center for Emerging Tropical Diseases and AIDS and a member of the Department of Virology and Developmental Genetics at Ben Gurion University. Professor Bentwich did an informal experiment with Uri in 1987, which is on record as the last known time Uri submitted to any kind of work in a laboratory. However, it did not go well.

Bentwich had been introduced to Uri as early as 1969 by his secretary, who happened to be Geller's old pilot friend Gideon Peleg's wife, Leah. 'What I saw Uri Geller do in the laboratory,' he attests, 'was a truly mind-blowing experience which cannot be overlooked, and should be made common knowledge once we have established it. I have no doubt that he manifests an extreme case of some unusual power, capacity or energy, which I believe is genuine and not magician- or performer-based – and which probably represents what all human beings have in much lower intensity.

'To start with, when we were younger,' Bentwich told me, 'I was impressed with the regular things he can do, the telepathy he showed me, the bending of spoons and the seed sprouting. What was most impressive in my mind was that the spoon continued to bend when it was clearly out of his touch. The seed sprouting, I found intriguing, rather than disturbing. I approached him at that time and asked him to give himself to further testing within our medical school, and I was amused by his almost paranoid reaction. He was extremely anxious at my suggestion. I felt there was something problematic in his coping with his powers not being under his control, in his attraction to show business, which I thought did him a big disservice.

'However, to my delight, in 1987, Uri agreed to come and be tested in my then laboratory, and at the Weizmann Institute, which is nearby.' [The postgraduate-only Weizmann Institute of Science is one of the world's top universities, rated by *The Scientist* magazine as the best place in the world to work in academia outside US institutions.]

'My colleagues and I designed three experiments to test if he has any special effects when he concentrates and puts his hands over a culture of cancer cells,' says Bentwich. 'The bottom line of these experiments was they were all negative, so there was another guy, an endocrinologist, who came in and said, "I have some ox sperm cells. Maybe this would affect the sperm."'

The sperm, Bentwich explains, were in frozen vials. 'They were put into a plate and were swimming around energetically, and then we had two similar culture plates that contained sperm in more or less the same amount as a control. Uri put his hand over one and, without touching it, concentrated. It was hot, in summer, so he wasn't wearing long sleeves or anything, and we checked out his hands for anything hidden. And, lo and behold, most of the sperm cells became either very slow in movement or died. We repeated this three times. It was very impressive, so we did it again and again. However, when he asked what it was we were doing and told him, he was extremely upset. He really thought he had a destructive power. This was a dramatic result, but he wasn't happy with it, and at that point, he said he didn't want to do anything more.

'After seeing such results, I told him: "Look we should continue testing. It is so interesting and amazing." But he didn't like the idea at all. At a later stage, I suggested that if he was concerned about negative forces, maybe we could try out some healing effects. He said that he liked that much more, but I didn't insist beyond a certain point, and we did nothing more, which I think is very regretful.

'I think Uri is a very fine person, Bentwich concluded. 'I like him personally, but in a way, I always considered him as an immature personality with an exceptional power that somehow he doesn't know how to cope with. He is attracted too much to showbiz and to performance, and not to more important things. Years have now gone by, and nobody has been studying him on any similar things, which is ridiculous. There was too little to go on, but what we had already seen was probably the most significant piece of evidence ever in

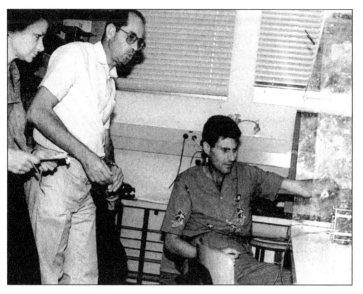

Uri in his last-ever laboratory test, in 1987, with Professor Zvi Bentwich in Israel.

terms of biological effect of what he is capable of, yet he refrained and said forget about me, try it with somebody else. He is far from being systematic. He is chaotic, so he didn't make the connection with AIDS and cancer, or even think about it. It was like missing the main point while looking round for nonsense.'

Chapter Nine

INTO THE 21ST CENTURY

A key Uri Geller characteristic, first seen back in Israel
when he was a young man, has continued unabated
into his 60s and the very different world of the early
21st century. This is his ability – surely unique – to mix his
spooky paranormal life with his crazy show business life with
his mysterious espionage life – and then to mix all three
with the serious, but non-clandestine, world of politics and
international relations.

In 2005, Uri played a key role – one publicly acknowledged
by the other participants – in cementing in Geneva a working
agreement between the Israeli and Palestinian versions of the
International Red Cross, the *Magen David Adom* (Red Star
of David) and the Palestine Red Crescent Society (founded
in 1968 by Yasser Arafat's brother, Fathi) respectively. Under
the agreement, the Israeli and the Palestinian organizations
officially recognized each other and would allow free passage
of medics and ambulances through each other's areas. The
Israeli ambulances would henceforth display a newly created,

politically and culturally neutral symbol known as the Red Crystal, with a small Star of David inside it. The Arab countries had previously objected to the Red Star of David's name and symbol because they argued the Jewish star was, since the foundation of Israel, a political emblem. The Red Crystal was also, as Uri told all concerned, of great resonance to him because he believes quartz crystals have special qualities. He always carries a couple in his pocket and has two giant crystals at the entrance to his house. Additionally, with the new arrangement in place, the *Magen David Adom* was accepted into the International Red Cross as a full member after 58 years of exclusion, rather than as observers, as had previously been the case. The Palestine Red Crescent likewise became fully affiliated to the International Committee of the Red Cross.

'Dr Noam Yifrach, head of Magen David Adom had for years been trying to get Israel into the International Red Cross,' Uri recalls of the extraordinary period leading up to the deal in November 2005. 'Yifrach had one day watched a *Reputations* documentary about me on BBC television. And when he saw that during the 1987 arms talks between the USA and the Soviet Union in Geneva, I had been brought in by the Americans to try to bombard the mind of Yuli Vorontsov, the head of the Soviet negotiating team, he said, "Wow! If Uri could do that, maybe we could use his talent to get us into the Red Cross."

'So Yifrach called me up and said he wanted to talk to me. I assumed he was looking for a donation, but he said, "No we don't want any money from you. We want something quite different and quite difficult to achieve." So I was intrigued and invited him to my house in Berkshire. He came with his deputy and said, "Look, Uri, we are negotiating with the Palestinians to get us and them accepted for the first time into the International Red Cross, but we are at a point where I think we need your help." So I said, "Yes, I'm sure I can help." I liked the idea of helping. I have lots of Muslim friends and I respect all religions, so this appealed a lot. But I said that first of all, he would have to make me legally something in his organization. So they activated their lawyers and officially made me the President of the Friends of *Magen David Adom*. With that done, we flew to the State Department in Washington, we went to Korea, and gradually I started to be introduced to the Palestinians in Ramallah, especially to the head of the Palestine Red Crescent, Younis Al-Khatib.

'So, soon the next round in the negotiations was beginning, all orchestrated by Jakob Kellenberger, who was head of the International Committee of the Red Cross and his team, and the head of the American Red Cross, Bonnie McElveen-Hunter. It was proving very difficult, however, to speak with the Palestinians. They were continually raising questions that were difficult for our team to answer, especially about Israeli checkpoints and about injured and pregnant people being stopped at the checkpoints when they are going to hospital and so on. But anyway, I said, "Yes, we will stop that. We will remove the checkpoints if we come to an agreement." But then they also wanted Red Crescent ambulances to operate in Jerusalem, and that gets even more political. To have an ambulance with a Red Crescent logo in Jerusalem would be tricky. Then they said, "Well your doctors are also carrying weapons in the ambulances." So there were a lot of negotiating problems to get through and a lot of ups and downs, and it was all pretty much stalled.

'But then after all the flying round the world we had done, at one meeting in the dining room of the Swiss Foreign Ministry in Bern with the Palestinian officials and dignitaries, I could see that things really weren't going anywhere and I said quietly to Shipi, "Hey, tell the *maître d'* to bring me a spoon." Micheline Calmy-Rey, the Swiss Foreign Minister, who was later President of Switzerland, was there and was smiling. I figured that the Palestinians don't know who I am or what I do, so maybe this was something worth trying to change the atmosphere for the better. And the headwaiter comes in with a spoon on a silver tray. I pick up the spoon and I bend it. And I hand it to Younis Al-Khatib and he freaks out because it continues bending in his hand. And they go into a huddle, I can hear they're talking about the supernatural and powers and someone is saying, "You see, that's why we have to talk", and suddenly, it all took off. They were all laughing and smiling, and it was like the whole Berlin Wall was dismantled at once. The negotiations were working.

'But meanwhile,' Uri continues, 'we were being inundated with people from the Israeli Foreign Ministry, watching us, wanting to know how can we allow Red Crescent ambulances into Jerusalem. But in the end the government officials said to us, "Yes, you can sign," and a big press conference was arranged for early the next morning for Noam Yifrach to sign with Younis Al-Khatib. But suddenly, very, very late at night, the Israeli side start saying they can't give us the OK without Prime Minister Ariel Sharon himself agreeing. We knew the documents were on his desk in Jerusalem, but by now it was 4am in Geneva, there were four hours to go before the signing, and they weren't willing to wake Sharon at 5am [in Israel]. They were insistent that they couldn't.

'But then Shipi remembered that Bonnie McElveen-Hunter had given us her mobile number and I jumped on the phone. We dialled her and luckily, she had her mobile on because it was about midnight in the USA. And I said, "Bonnie, you've got to pull a miracle, the Israelis are giving us problems now. You've got to call the White House and wake up President Bush and ask him to get you Ariel Sharon's personal number. I know him, I can call him, but I don't have his number."

'So she finds a number from the White House – I believe they actually did wake up Bush or an immediate aide for it – and pulls off exactly the miracle we had asked her for. She called us back with Sharon's number. So we called Sharon and the government officials tell him that he's the only person who can give the green light to Yifrach to sign. And Ariel Sharon goes to his desk, sits down and spends an hour looking at everything, calls the Foreign Ministry and tells them it's OK, they can sign. So now, if Israeli ambulances have to go into Gaza, or Palestinian ambulances in Jerusalem, they have the red crystal, which isn't a religious symbol like the Star of David, or the crescent, or the cross. There's also an agreement now that Palestinian ambulances are fast-tracked through checkpoints if they are carrying injured people or pregnant women. They called it The Third Protocol, this Red Crystal.'

Acclaim for Uri's success at 'bending' the negotiations came from the highest quarters. Micheline Calmy-Rey said in a speech to the assembled dignitaries: 'Uri Geller did not just help break the ice with the skills that have made him famous – a considerable number of bent spoons line the road that led to this agreement. He has also played a pivotal role in helping everyone focus on the main objective and overcoming differences over secondary details at key junctures.' Bonnie McElveen-Hunter also acknowledged Uri's role back in the States.

Over the years, interesting new snippets of information, concerning Uri's abilities and his covert work have continued to slip out – or be ferreted out by the dogged new breed of Internet-powered researchers with various fields of interest. Some of the work of these people, is, perhaps, tinged at the edges with obsession, but we will briefly look at a few of the more plausible nuggets that have been unearthed.

In November 2007, in a lengthy and meticulously researched re-examination of Uri by Brendan Burton, a UK-based founder and co-administrator of a body called the Open Minds Forum, appeared in the online *American Chronicle*. The OMF includes astroscientists, biologists, psychologists, journalists, theologians, forensic experts and other professionals, and is particularly interested in the UFO issue.

Among Burton's fascinating findings and observations were some that have since been confirmed by the BBC documentary maker, Vikram Jayanti. Burton firmed up the rumour, for example, that the CIA continued working with Russell Targ and Hal Puthoff for many years after their SRI work with Uri, suggesting, as Burton says – and crucially, this is before the key CIA man, Kit Green, came forward –that even if there were some doubts in the scientific world about the pair's SRI work, the CIA saw no problems with it.

Burton also reported that he had asked Dr Jack Sarfatti, an American theoretical physicist who has supported Uri since the 1970s, to discuss the ability to bend metals by mind power. 'I have seen things in my trip to Brazil in 1985 shown to me by a General in the Brazilian army, allegedly from a UFO that landed in the Amazon jungle, that is like what Uri did with metal but even more complex than what I saw Uri do in 1974,' Burton quotes Sarfatti as saying.

Burton also had one of the last interviews with the metallurgist and US Naval scientist, Eldon Byrd, before Byrd's death in 2002. He asked Byrd for his most up-to-date knowledge of psychokinesis. 'I developed several theories about how PK might work in the metal-bending phenomena,' Byrd said. 'As a physical scientist I have always been more interested in phenomena that produce hard analysable data, rather than the soft statistical pabulum [meaning bland or insipid intellectual material] of parapsychology. Recently, I have become acquainted with new information on how the mind can interact with biological processes; I have altered my previous theories. That is how science progresses – not with "proof", but by coherency. We are close to understanding how intention can create action at a distance.'

'In respect of Geller,' Brendan Burton wrote, 'there is too much credible witness evidence to suggest that he is just employing mere trickery. Indeed, if such were the case, he would be perhaps even more of a phenomenal person, having maintained a level of deceit so powerful it has managed to fool some of the most credible academics in history, people with high-level security clearances, physicists, metallurgists, astronauts, magicians, politicians and world leaders, in short, the kind of people we tend to invest our trust into. Such supposed "trickery" to such a large and grand scale has certainly never been done before, and leads even some of the most sceptical to consider: "This can't be possible … can it?"'

Burton concluded: 'Sceptics often claim that these people are not expert at recognizing the tricks and tools of deception, yet how do we explain the witness accounts of some of the world's finest stage magicians, also seeing the first hand "bending" phenomena? The testimony of these people alone shows that Uri Geller is perhaps NOT the "parlour-trick" charlatan some pseudo-sceptics claim.'

Another writer fascinated by Uri but more so by Dr Andrija Puharich, the esoteric author Phillip Coppens, has been continuing his lifelong research on Puharich and concluding that the mysterious Serbian-American was very probably a CIA agent on a long-term, if eccentrically executed, mission to investigate Uri. 'Uri Geller stated in 1996 that he "probably" believed that "the whole thing with Andrija was financed by the American Defense Department,"' wrote Coppens on his website. That opinion was also expressed by Jack Sarfatti, who added that Puharich was Geller's case officer in America, with money provided by a British philanthropist.

The evidence, Coppens concluded, is that Puharich's ultimate mission was to discredit Uri's powers, or at least to turn them into an unverifiable myth and disinform the public. 'Why? Perhaps Puharich did not want the paradigm shift to happen after all. But perhaps (more likely) he was following orders, and the orders were that the status quo had to remain. It seems a logical enough assumption that the US government was not interested in paradigm shifts, but instead preferred status quo, in which the [evidence of the] existence of ESP was contained within the corridors of their own buildings, and not displayed in every street of the world. With such a paradigm shift, there was more than the state of the family silverware at stake.'

Another possibly significant new reworking of old evidence, on Gary S. Bekkum's STARpod website, followed up a line on Uri discovered by the respected British author and documentary maker Jon Ronson while researching his 2004 book, *The Men Who Stare At Goats*, which was subsequently made into a Hollywood film. Ronson discovered from Uri, that, following the 9/11 attacks, he had been reactivated by the 'Ron' we read about earlier into the ranks of intelligence agency psychic spies to help track the movement of terrorists and weapons of mass destruction.

'Based on information provided to us by various sources,' Bekkum's site reported, 'we strongly suspect that Ron is a former high-ranking CIA agency analyst, previously tasked to monitor technology developments in China. The big question remains: which intelligence agencies might be involved in the latest version of a psychic black ops antiterrorist unit? MASINT (Measurement and Signatures Intelligence) is a likely candidate, but our present understanding is that Ron is working for John Negroponte at the Department of National Intelligence.' [This analysis does not rule out Ron Pandolfi, a former colleague of Kit Green, who has often been assumed – incorrectly, says Green – to be 'Ron'.]

'Rumours persist that America's DIA trained psychic-intelligence sources are viewing mushroom clouds over numerous cities in the homeland. Taken in tandem with the constant rumours of loose nukes, it appears that the psychic spies have been reactivated, at least in part, by the man said to have had a hand in shutting down the original DIA Stargate psychic spy-program,' Bekkum's article continued.

'All in all it would seem that there is something about space, time and beyond that we don't understand. Researchers have discovered mirror neurons that empathetically fire in your brain when you are watching someone else get poked by a needle, for example. Somehow the neurons in a remote viewer must fire empathetically for information about distant events, removed from ordinary sensory detection.

'Last year,' the article concluded, 'the [US] Air Force received a great deal of flak from the press about a research paper they commissioned to examine the use of teleportation for military purposes. Apparently the journalists didn't realize that quantum teleportation has been an active area of mainstream research, ever since it was discovered by a team at IBM in the 1990s. MIT professor Seth Lloyd has been researching the use of quantum teleportation for communication networks. Lloyd's support includes DARPA, the Defense Advanced Research Projects Agency. Recently he also developed an interest in quantum gravity, the elusive theory that would unite Einstein's theory of bending space and time with the foundation stone of all modern electronics and atomic engineering: the quantum theory.'

Heady stuff, perhaps off-the-wall stuff. But in the meantime, what, in 2013, does Uri Geller now believe he is, and what do his powers consist of? He was, after all to a large extent, the catalyst, in the West at least, for the whole business of involving psychics and remote viewers with the espionage and defence arenas.

'In the 1970s,' Geller says today, 'if you asked me, "What are you?" I immediately said, "I'm a psychic." But I know PR, and I realized it was important to go with the flow and reinvent myself, so later I began calling myself a paranormalist and more recently, a mystifier. And that is the truth: I've mystified millions of people. I've mystified them for more than 60 years. But I still say, because it's true, that I have supernatural powers. I'm real. I'm authentic and genuine. I believe we all have psychic powers and we are intuitive in nature and that infuriates some sceptics and magicians.

Uri is warming to his newly coined, self-affixed 'mystifier' label. His favourite quote today from the (often over-quoted) Albert Einstein is this: 'The most beautiful thing we can experience is the mysterious. It is the source of all true art and science. He to whom the emotion is a stranger, who can no longer pause to wonder and stand wrapped in awe, is as good as dead – his eyes are closed.'

So is the new 'mystifier' idea a sign of Geller backing down over any part of his paranormal claims? 'No, you just have to be flexible in life. You have to compromise. That's show business,' he says. 'I respect all magicians tremendously and I'm flattered by the fact that I influenced a whole new generation of mentalists. Of course some of the sceptics jump on my words now. Some sceptics still lie and invent things about me. They still make up stories … you know the kind of thing, that he had a magnet on his thumb when he moved the compass. There's a YouTube video showing me in Israel, the sceptics say, with a magnet on my thumb – actually a false magnetic thumb that, according to them, I kept hidden in my hair. Can you imagine me doing that when eight cameras are rolling? I'm not that stupid. But they believe what they want to believe these people, they see exactly what they want to see. For my part, I loved it that 1.4 million people clicked to watch that video. It's all amazing publicity, and it's still going on nearly 50 years on from when I started professionally.'

Geller is actually proud to point out that just one of the multiple postings on YouTube of a video of him failing (rather than cheating) on the Johnny Carson show in 1973 has been viewed by 3.2m people in six years. 'That's like filling the Yankee Stadium 64 times,' he says. 'Or if each of those people has watched the 14-minute video, it means they have collectively invested 31,000 days, or 85 years in watching a derogatory video about me. For my part, I say I don't really care what they say about me, so long as they spell my name correctly. It's all free publicity. I don't even read it, I just measure it.'

When asked if he knows today any more than he did when we first used to discuss his powers how he does it, he replied, 'No. I still don't. It just happens.' 'But let's just say I am the greatest magician in the world, and I did manage to do all this for nearly 60 years with hidden chemicals, by sleight of hand or with mirrors.

'I think the amazing thing that has happened over these many years is not the science of it, but the fact that I have brought this kind of phenomenon, into modern culture. People didn't believe in miracles any more, in inexplicable things. But then I brought in this simple, everyday icon of a bending spoon – a simple little thing like a spoon – and years later, you're watching a massive Hollywood production, *The Matrix,* and when Keanu Reeves walks into the Oracle these children teach him how to bend a spoon.

'The little boy in the scene bends a spoon and straightens it out again before handing it to Reeves and says, "Do not try and bend the spoon, it's impossible. Instead, only try to realize the truth." Reeves asks, "What truth?" And the boy replies, "There is no spoon." Reeves responds, puzzled, "There is no spoon?" The boy comes back, "Then you will see, it is not the spoon that bends, it is only yourself." And with that, Reeves stares long and hard at the spoon, before it appears to bend for him, too.

'And that's not the only appearance of spoon bending in popular culture,' Uri continues. 'Kenny Rogers sings about spoon bending. Johnny Cash and Michael Stipe of R.E.M. both mention it. Robert de Niro played a sinister version of me in *Red Light*. Incubus mention me in their hit song, *Nice To Know You*. I'm even mentioned by Woody Allen in *Annie Hall*. I've been on a Pokemon card as a character called Un-Geller. Oh, and IKEA brought out a chair with twisted legs, that they called URI. I'm trying not to sound as if I'm bragging, but it's just amazing to me how this simple thing has become a little part of the culture.'

In recent years, Uri has hosted TV shows in several countries, aimed at finding a 'new' Uri Geller, and appropriately called *The Successor*. The first, in Israel, was won by a young magician called Lior. So does Uri believe that people like Lior, have paranormal powers? 'The thing is,' Uri says, 'I'm not a magician. I don't know anything about magic effects or tricks. So when I see them perform, I don't know how they do it. I'm watching them like I'm one of the people at home watching. Before the show goes on, I always meet the contestants and say, "Listen, guys, don't worry when you see me sitting there. Don't think that I know how you do it because I don't."

'So the truth is, I don't know whether Lior has supernatural powers. This show isn't about whether you're real or not. I want to believe he has supernatural powers but I don't know. He may be a great mentalist. David Berglas [the outstanding British magician and former chairman of The Magic Circle] says about me, "If Uri is a magician, then he is the best we have ever seen, and the most famous since Houdini. On the other hand, if he is a psychic then he is the only man who can do what he does. Magician or psychic, agree or disagree with him, either way we have to respect him for what he has done. He is truly a phenomenon."

'The Successor is not a scientific show, it's pure entertainment and in the press conference in Moscow, before the Russian version, I made it absolutely clear to everyone that this is the case. I think more and more that there doesn't really need to be this divide between whether performers are psychic or not. The question is unlikely to be resolved in the near future. The phenomena are too fleeting and subtle to categorize by traditional methodology. The more sophisticated commentators like Berglas understand that there is a wide grey area in all this. Marcello Truzzi [the academic and former leading sceptic who became a firm friend of Uri] understood this, too. Marcello never ever "believed" in my talent or my gifts or my powers, but he was always with me. He was an honest, non-vicious man, a real friend to me.

'People sometime ask if my powers are diminishing with age, and the answer is, no, I am actually experiencing these days a surge of energy that I've never had. And all around me, these crazy things keep happening all the time. I'm still bending spoons, making them fly off television sets in people's homes. So I'm more inclined today to believe that there is a thinking entity behind all this. So the Puharich tales, the Lawrence Livermore voices, the tapes materializing, the voices appearing on the tapes, they're all beginning to fall into place now. And I do feel that there is definitely some kind of intelligent energy involved here that is possibly directing me, or all of us.'

In this new, more contemplative and relaxed phase of his life, Uri has been quietly developing, year on year, a more textured, nuanced theory of his and others' inexplicable powers. On the one hand, he has, so it seems, come to an accommodation (up to a point) with the conventional magic world. Once he might have been offended by it because of the name of the magazine, but today, he is proud of a statement that appeared in the journal *Magic* in the USA in May 2008: 'Continuing what has to be one of the biggest comebacks in modern times,' the piece read, 'Uri Geller successfully continues his conquest of worldwide television.'

On the other hand, Uri's spiritual side seems to be maturing apace. In his 1999 book *Mind Medicine* he summed up in a particularly interesting and profound way what this 'mind power' might consist of. He wrote: 'I believe it represents a deep wisdom that we all inherit form our forebears and which, once harnessed, can effectively give every one of us much greater knowledge and insight into out lives. I believe that with such awareness comes healthier minds and bodies. Some of us learn how to tap into this energy earlier than others; some come upon it through trial and error. Others cannot explain it, but trust it totally. Its power is formidable and this frightens those who have not yet reached the point of understanding the potency of such an invisible force.'

Chapter Ten

SO?

Uri Geller's is, by any measure, a strange, strange story.

A grown man, of past statutory retirement age, who behaves like a bright, impatient, demanding, unreliable kid, can't get enough publicity, is almost wholly indiscriminating as to where it appears, shrugs it off when it leads to him being laughed at or ridiculed, but sees red and gets the most expensive lawyers in town involved if his honour – as opposed to his demeanour – is impugned.

Yet at the same time, this big teenager has a direct, earthy wisdom – many would say a guru quality – that some of the world's greatest and most prominent men and women of recent decades have respected and sought out. He has also been entrusted with significant state secrets, and, as we now know was used for decades as a *de facto* secret agent of one sort or another by the intelligence apparatus (or maybe rogue elements within these) of one superpower and another nuclear-armed nation.

The key things to appreciate about Uri Geller for people who do not know him well are, in the author's view, his integrity and trustworthiness. These, of course, are exactly the qualities that Geller's most fundamentalist detractors say he lacks, but we have dealt with them in previous chapters; they tend to be hardline, extreme, unbending materialist rationalists, who often take this position to the point, ironically, of irrationality. So much so that rationalists have been known to abandon sceptical organizations because of a disturbing fundamentalism within their ranks.

One is, by convention, allowed in the conclusion to a book like this to be a little personal and generalize, and if the author is to be allowed one massive oversimplification about Geller it is this: that, in his opinion, in spite of Uri's wholly obvious shortcomings, his inner circle of friends and defenders is characterized by their being intelligent, educated, pre-eminent in their field, worldly, intellectually curious, experienced – meaning, often older – iconoclastic, unconcerned about going with the herd, and in possession of the real X-factor – emotional intelligence.

This is no small point. It is often said by opponents of Geller that the weakness of his case for the paranormal is that he has problems producing effects if he is not happy, or is surrounded by people willing him to fail. One aspect of emotional intelligence, if one may generalize further, is that people who have it are receptive to the idea that all kinds of things, from athletic performance to, yes, physical phenomena *can* be enhanced by positive emotion. Practically every experienced doctor will attest to this when it comes to the effect of medical treatment. Mind absolutely can affect matter.

What Vikram Jayanti, in his groundbreaking 2013 BBC TV film on Geller referred to cleverly and amusingly – 'his Zelig-like ability to pop up in the highest political circles' is true, but the remarkable thing is that Uri is voluntarily invited into these circles in the first place. He may have proved a handy secret agent in his time, and seems to be still making himself useful in that respect, but he *is* capable of being discreet, and he does not tend to infiltrate the highest echelons without being asked.

So what about those who think he's a fraud, that his supernatural abilities are pie in the sky. They can't all be extremists, surely? Well, we live at a time when hard-nosed, white-lab-coat hyper-rationalism is fashionable across the Western secular world, and with that background, it is unquestionably the fact that across the broad span of the educated Western public, the Geller detractors are in the ascendant.

As a result, it's probably fair to say that the bulk of this demographic is sceptical to the point of cynicism about Uri. His love affair with the tabloid media and his often splashy publicity stunts do not help in that respect; he argues that he has a mission, as a working-class guy himself, to help show the regular person in the street that there might just be a world more interesting and mysterious than the daily grind. But this does not play well, by and large, with the graduate class, who are conditioned by seeing him described in pejorative terms, or just as a joke.

The one thing the author wishes he could impress upon this broad, educated elite is that, while there are undoubtedly lunatics and unfortunate acolytes among Uri's 'fanbase', there is, among the committed 'professional' sceptics (as opposed to people who question all received wisdom, which is obviously a wholly admirable trait) an extraordinary level of seemingly panic-stricken propagandizing that rears its head whenever they discuss him. Significant figures in organized sceptical circles truly *hate* Uri Geller. They tell easily exposed lies about him. They propose implausible explanations and conspiracy theories about how he does what he does. And they swamp anyone interested with misinformation.

They also, and it's not a stupid tactic, enrol professional magicians to debunk Geller, and snigger that the scientists who worked with him were naïve and were hoodwinked by him and Shipi. One problem here is that the experiments, especially at SRI, were heavily supervised by magicians specializing in mentalist effects. The story of the scientists being conned simply does not stand up. Another issue for the sceptics is that there is in fact far from a consensus among magicians that Uri is just a production-line conjuror and an unprincipled scoundrel, too. There were many magicians stung from the first by the raw originality of Geller. But many others support him to varying degrees. We have already read the view of David Berglas, a former President of the Magic Circle, that if Geller is a magician, he is the best in history.

Here is a younger, more current magician, David Blaine on Uri: 'Uri bent a spoon for me. The first time he did it, I thought there must be a trick. The second time I was stunned, completely, completely stunned and amazed. It just bent in my hand. I've never seen anything like it. It takes a lot to impress me. Uri Geller is for real and anyone who doesn't recognize that is either deluding himself, or is a very sad person.' And here is David Copperfield: 'You know, I like Uri Geller. He is a good guy. I think he made many things with

Uri and cult American magician David Blaine, who flew to Britain just after he started out to meet his childhood hero.

his abilities. I think some of the things he shows are illusion. But I cannot claim for sure, that this applies to everything.' (You can read other commendations from magicians on Uri's website – www.urigeller.com)

Another issue successfully fogged by sceptics is the question of scientific testing. As was pointed out in Chapter 2, you will often hear people say authoritatively that Geller has never been examined dispassionately by a reputable scientist. Hopefully, this untruth can be finally laid to rest with the evidence in this book, and also, perhaps, by the almost relentless list of scientists' quotes on Uri's site.

Does Uri Geller have unexplained powers? A lot of exceptionally smart and eminent scientists say so. Has he been a part-time secret agent for almost his entire entertainment career? A number of spymasters, arguably mavericks themselves, say so. The sheer bulk of government intelligence agencies in the USA and Israel that have taken him seriously is startling. So, yes, there is ample evidence that he really has been a spy, and by certain readings of this evidence, a fairly potent double and triple agent too. And with that it mind, it's fair to ask whether he has over the years used trickery to *fool* us all into thinking he was just a rather ham-fisted magician, rather than someone with legitimate powers.

Among many other questions that remain unanswered about Uri Geller is, if he has always been just a straight magician, why did he not expand his repertoire? It's quite a career decision to make at 19 and stick with for the rest of your life to restrict yourself to spoon bending and mind reading and deliberately do nothing else.

For him to be a fraud all along would have involved Uri lying to his children throughout their entire lifetime. There are arguments around this, that once a person is defined by a lie, it's hard to extract him or her from it. But for a family man like Uri, it would have been a big ask. An impossible ask, in all probability.

Are Geller's abilities real, but no more than a highly developed version of something we can all do – and perhaps used to do more in the past, or will do more in the future? It sounds a bit of a hippy-dippy argument, but it has its scientific supporters. Here is the Argentine-born quantum physicist – and philosopher – Dr George Weissmann, who studied at Imperial College, London, gained a PhD in Theoretical Physics at the University of California, Berkeley in 1978, studying high energy physics. Weissmann's thesis appeared across the best part of two issues of the *International Journal of Theoretical Physics* (Vol 17 No 10, and No 11). He went on to do postdoctoral research at the Swiss Federal Institute of Technology in Zurich.

Weissmann has spent decades fathoming the mysteries within mysteries of quantum, but, after explaining that, while he thinks Geller's abilities are indubitably real and have clearly been tested to the most rigorous of standards, he argues that they are not wholly – or even partly – explicable by quantum entanglement because of the strange role of will and intention manifest in 'the Geller effect'.

'I want to put the Uri Geller phenomenon in a larger context,' Dr Weissmann told the author in 2013. 'He is a true master of *psi*, but *psi* is a basic human faculty which we all have to some extent; however, our culture and its belief system has suppressed these faculties in most of us to the point where we are no longer in touch with them and sometimes don't even believe in their existence.'

'That being said, Uri is still a giant in this field. It is like saying that everyone who has some lessons can play the piano to some extent, which is true; but very few will become pianists, and very, very few will be a Rubinstein or Horowitz. Uri is the champion. But it is more truthful and more appropriate to present him as a master of something that we are all potentially capable of, and can learn to some degree. In other words, Uri is a master rather than a freak. There may be special reasons why Uri is so much more talented than most; he has talked about his contact with ETs and maybe attributed his special gifts to this contact, but the fact remains that he is an outlier genius rather than a unique phenomenon.'

The last word, as many would think apt, comes from a leading sceptic, the Liverpool University psychologist Graham Wagstaff, renowned in recent years for arguing that hypnosis does not exist. The author has long been intrigued by this story Wagstaff told him many years ago, because of the way it explains, for him, how some people are interested in 'mysteries', while others just are not.

Wagstaff believes that we all have stories the likes of which Geller and those interested in the paranormal are fascinated by, but that a *proper* sceptic retains his scepticism at pretty much all costs.

'We all have these experiences,' Wagstaff said. 'One of my favourites was when the wing mirror on my car got mended by itself. It was in about 1975, when I lived in Newcastle, and, no, I wasn't on drugs. I had a Ford Anglia, and the mirror was dangling off. Then one morning, I came along and it wasn't dangling off. It was mended.

'That's how I remember it. I'd looked at it, and I couldn't see how anyone could fix it. Yet I'm not suggesting that anything weird and wonderful happened – just that, I suppose, I must have seen it wrong, or I'd made some sort of mistake, or my memory was playing tricks on me or something like that. I went through everything. None of the neighbours knew what had happened. I was quite worried about it. It's quite *possible* that some good Samaritan mended it, but I would have thought it was beyond repair. It was hanging down.'

'But,' he concluded, 'I'm a real sceptic, so there must be some explanation.'

INDEX

Illustrations are given in *italics*.

257

Index

Index